In 1979, Rusty Rosenberger shocked the world by defeating Reggie Jones to become the New Jersey Middleweight Boxing Champion. The World Title was within his grasp—he believed it was destiny. Then, his manager, Lou Duva, slipped him some pills before a match. How could he take the beating that followed?

This book is about the worst that men can do, and how a man can stand back up and fight after he's been knocked down. It's for anyone who's into the sport of boxing, and especially for anyone who needs a hero. Rusty offers a deeply personal look into the life and times of a true contender.

UNCLAIMED DESTINY
THE HEART OF A CHAMPION

Copyright © 2003 Rusty Rosenberger
ISBN: 1-894942-13-2
Cover art by Marlies Bugmann, design by Martine Jardin

All rights reserved. Except for use in any review, the reproduction or utilization of this work in whole or in part in any form by any electronic, mechanical or other means, now known or hereafter invented, is forbidden without the written permission of the publisher.

Published by Zumaya Publications, 2003
Look for us online at: www.zumayapublications.com

UNCLAIMED DESTINY

THE HEART OF A CHAMPION

BY

RUSTY ROSENBERGER

DEDICATION

To my lovely wife, Cindy, the angel God sent to watch over me. I will always love you and my children.

ACKNOWLEDGEMENTS

Thanks to Cindy. Without her, this book would never have been. Thanks to Jeff, Liz, Tina and all the wonderful people at Zumaya Publishing. Without them, I never would have had a chance to let people know what happened.

CHAPTER ONE

POT OF GOLD

Some of the best fighters in the world come out of the state of New Jersey. Though I had fought in only one four- and twelve six-round undefeated bouts, I still earned the rating of the number-one ranked middleweight in the state of New Jersey. I was pleased to have won such a prestigious title, but I was not satisfied nor would I be until I reached my true destiny as the Middleweight Champ of the World.

Living up to my reputation as a "boxer-puncher," I displayed excellent footwork, threw good combinations and developed good hand speed and punching power. I had an outstanding jab, a one-punch knockout right hand and a left hook to match. Most of my knockouts came when I landed a perfectly timed right hand on the chin—"the phantom punch," first made famous by Muhammad Ali. I went to the body well, and my slip game made me virtually impossible to hit with a clean punch.

Still, I didn't let it go to my head. I totally dedicated myself to becoming not just good, but the best of the best.

Learning fast and loving to train, I continued striving to realize my destiny as the World Middleweight Champ. By April of 1979, I had compiled an impressive record of thirteen wins, no losses, with eight knockouts.

Aside from being my manager, Lou Duva also served as the president of a Teamster's Union local in New Jersey. He held that influential position for fifteen years. He told me, "If you keep winning and looking as impressive as you have in your previous fights, you could end up fighting Reggie Jones (the 1972 Olympic Silver Medalist) for the Middleweight State Championship of New Jersey."

Lou arranged for us to go and watch Reggie Jones defend his title against a fighter by the name of Ray Kates, a co-feature fight on a boxing card held at the Rahway State Penitentiary in Rahway, New Jersey. It was a nationally televised show, and the main event featured a real rugged fighter and an inmate of Rahway by the name of James Scott. Of course, we saw it live.

When we walked into the prison, the guards immediately patted us down. I guess they didn't want anyone bringing in contraband. We strolled down a makeshift hallway constructed of two chain link fences that acted like walls on each side to keep the civilians separated from the inmate population. Several black inmates climbed up on this fence and just hung there. They started yelling weird stuff at us, like "Hey, cutie, what's your name? Can I call you later?"

Lou and I got through that part okay, and found our seats. By then, it was time for the co-feature, Reggie Jones vs. Ray Kates. Before the two warriors entered the ring, the announcer took time out to introduce some of the celebrities sitting at ringside: first, New Jersey State boxing commissioner Robert Lee, then Guy (The Rock) Cassle, a heavyweight contender. To my surprise and delight, he introduced me as the number-one ranked middleweight in

New Jersey. It gave me a feeling of finally being someone special.

Everyone in the arena applauded, I stood up and raised my hand in the air over my head and it felt good. I remember saying to myself, if I get this kind of response being the number-one contender, just think of the attention I'll get when I'm the champ, It ignited a new fire deep in my soul. That kind of attention when I went somewhere, anywhere, was just what I wanted. I told myself on that day, *I will be the champ.*

While watching Mr. Jones defending his title, I studied his style. When he came forward and he had his opponent backing up, he controlled the tempo. He threw a powerful left hook, and his build reminded me of the one-time heavyweight champ, "Smokin Joe" Frazier. He even fought much the same, always the aggressor, pressing the action. Jones wore down his opponent.

In that fight, his tactics worked. He trapped Mr. Kates a number of times on the ropes or in the corners each round and banged away, almost at will. At the end of the twelfth round, the referee raised Reggie's hand in victory as the announcer called out, "The winner and still New Jersey Middleweight State Champ, Reggie Jones."

I felt confident after watching Reggie fight that if given the chance to fight him I could do well or at least give him a run for his money. During one of our many conversations, Lou told me, "The best way to move a young talent up the ladder is you get him experience fighting as many rounds as possible, gradually, not all at once. Start him off fighting four-round fights, then six, eight, ten, and then put him in a twelve-round championship fight."

Less than a month had gone by when Lou contradicted himself. Without my knowledge or consent, he told me, "I've signed a contract for you to fight for the New Jersey Middleweight Championship against Reggie Jones."

I was in total shock, being concerned about fighting for the title. I'd be going into untested waters against a Silver Medalist in the Olympics and a world-class fighter, with experience going twelve rounds on more than one occasion.

Lou encouraged me. "Don't worry, I'll get you a good trainer from New York City by the name of Chickie Farrah, an old-timer who for many years trained fighters. He'll teach you a lot of the 'old tricks of the trade.' To name just two, Chickie's impressive list of past clientele includes Earnie Shavers and Roberto Duran."

I was to work under Chickie's direction at the famed Gleason's Gym in New York City.

My training included a five-mile run up and down Garrett Mountain in West Patterson, New Jersey. I lived there in an apartment complex, nestled in the side of the mountain. Every morning, via a winding road, I'd run to the very top, where a parking lot awaited my arrival and offered a commanding view of Manhattan. The World Trade Center looked tall and majestic as the buildings towered over all the other skyscrapers in the New York City skyline.

When I reached the top, I'd jump up and down and yell, "I'm the champ, I'm the champ of the world," shadowbox for about five minutes then run back down.

On the third day of training, it was a bright, beautiful, cool early-spring morning. While I was running, a West Patterson policeman pulled up beside me in his squad car. He asked me why I was running at seven o'clock in the morning. I told him of my upcoming championship fight. From that moment on, he became a fan of Rusty Rosenberger, and a friend.

I remember that day so well because a few minutes after I finished talking with the sergeant, continuing my run, I stepped in a hole in the road and twisted my left knee. For the next three days, when I ran in the morning, I'd run about a mile and my knee would begin to feel like someone stuck a knife into it. I stopped running and walked a short distance, then tried running again. Ran about a quarter of a mile, and my knee began to hurt again.

When Lou picked me up to take me to the gym later that same day, I told him of my accident.

"Give it a couple of days, if it still bothers you, I'll take you to get it checked out by a doctor friend of mine," he responded. Being the president of a Teamster's local, he knew a lot of people in almost every kind of business.

A few days passed, and still my knee bothered me when I ran. Lou never took me to see his doctor friend. Instead, he suggested, "To make up for the roadwork you miss, jump rope an extra round or two in the gym at the end of a training session."

I did as Lou told me. In fact, I always did as he said, because I trusted him completely. I felt he cared for me and wanted to see me become champ. Besides, a boxer can't do everything by himself. I would spar eight rounds a day, hit the heavy bag four rounds, the speed bag three rounds. I then put myself through a marathon session of jumping rope, thirty minutes straight, every day, five days a week, for three weeks. It really strengthened my legs and got me in great condition. Jumping rope didn't bother my injured knee.

On more than one occasion I remember Lou asking me, "Are you doing any roadwork?"

I told him no, I couldn't, my knee still hurt. Immediately, he cracked a smile. I never understood why that made him happy.

Lou hired me a sparring partner, a guy named Bobby Patterson. Bobby'd fought Reggie a year or two earlier for the title but lost. I picked him up every day in downtown Patterson, where he lived, to take him to the gym with me for a workout sparring session.

We drove into New York City via the Lincoln Tunnel; and, as I was a kid from Ohio, that in itself impressed me. We parked in a parking lot just around the corner from the gym. If instead of turning to the right to go to Gleason's Gym we had turned left, we could have walked right into Madison Square Garden.

Every fighter dreams of fighting at the Garden. That dream came true for me—almost. It was earlier in my career—my eleventh fight, to be precise. I had fought at the Felt Forum, not at the main arena in the Garden, but close enough.

In preparation for my title fight one Saturday morning, I arrived at Gleason's Gym early, got dressed in my workout clothes and ended up in one of the two rings loosening up by shadow boxing. I was dancing around in the ring, throwing punches at an imaginary opponent, facing the back wall of the gym. When I turned around to continue my shadow boxing, I could not believe my eyes. The gym had somehow become packed full of people. How could all these people enter the gym in such a hurry? I didn't even hear or see them coming in.

Why did all these people come here? I wondered. I ignored them and kept loosening up. Then I heard the crowd let out a cheer.

For me? I thought. *No, but…why?*

I turned, and I was met head-on by Roberto Duran, the Lightweight Champ of the World. He said to me in broken English, "Box."

Mr. Duran and I shadowboxed for three rounds. I must have impressed him, because he asked me to spar with him. Being totally overwhelmed by the "Hands of Stone's" presence, being unquestionably intimidated and in total awe of this great fighter, I respectfully told him, "No, thanks."

On another day I met another boxer who was also a middleweight. We sparred only two rounds on the day we met but made a date to train with each other on the following Saturday.

I arrived at the gym early as I always did and ended up in one of the two rings shadow boxing and loosening up in preparation for a sparring session. I waited for him for about a half hour when in walks his girlfriend. She advised me that Tony couldn't make it that day.

"He has an audition for a possible TV show."

I replied, "Really, what is the name of the TV show he's trying to audition for?"

She said, "It's a show called *Taxi*."

Tony Danza never did hook up with me to spar, and the result of that audition is TV history.

It was one week before my title fight with Reggie Jones, scheduled for April 27, 1979, at the Robert Treat Hotel in downtown Newark, New Jersey. The promoters of the championship fight show called themselves "Triangle Productions." They were a group of Black Muslims, which Reggie belonged to. They arranged for the World Middleweight Champ Huggo Corro's attorney to fly to Newark from Argentina to attend our press conference. Originally, I didn't know why he chose to attend.

"What reason would he have to fly all this way to be at our press conference?" I asked Lou.

"Don't worry about it," he replied. "It's nothing."

Before I was given the honor of being introduced to the press, the New Jersey Boxing Commissioner, Robert Lee, made an announcement that took me by surprise. Huggo Corro's attorney had traveled all that distance to present Reggie Jones with a contract for a projected upcoming title fight with Huggo Corro. The contract read, "If Reggie Jones beats Rusty Rosenberger one week from the signing of this contract for the New Jersey Middleweight State Championship, Reggie Jones will be guaranteed a World Title fight against Huggo Corro for the Middleweight

Championship of the World."

Man, I was in shock. They even asked me to sign their contract as a witness to the fight deal between Reggie Jones and Huggo Curro, which I did.

Again I asked Lou, "Did you know about this ahead of time?"

"Yeah," he said, "don't let bother you. It's just a publicity stunt in case Reggie beats you. Just don't worry about it, you'll be okay."

Finally, it was my turn for some of the spotlight. I was introduced to the media as the number-one challenger for Reggie's title. Two of the newspaper reporters that showed up to cover our press conference asked me about Reggie's signing for a world title fight. Did that impress me or have any kind of impact on the upcoming fight?

My reply was simple and to the point. I told them, "The contract states, if he beats me he'll be guaranteed the title fight, right? Well, in my book that's a big 'if,' because he'll have to do just that—beat me. I'm not going to lie down and quit."

I received a positive reaction from the reporters, though they didn't publish any of my comments in the papers the following day. The papers all focused on Reggie and his upcoming world title fight with Huggo Curro. They didn't even consider me part of the equation. I didn't matter, being such a heavy underdog with the bookies. They gave me only two chances of winning—slim and none—since I had never fought nor did Lou ever schedule me to fight more than a six-round fight.

At the time, I was considered a six-round club fighter. No one in their right mind ever thought I should last more than eight rounds. I would start getting tired; and Reggie, having the edge and experience fighting twelve-round fights, should be able to stop me with his powerful left hooks and superior conditioning.

The press conference neared the end. Reggie approached me and pointed his index finger in my face, telling me, "I'm going to teach you a lesson you'll not soon forget, Rosenburg."

Then, he tried to poke me in my chest with his extended finger. He thrust his pointed finger at me. I took a quick step backwards, making him miss his target; and he lost his balance briefly. I looked him in the eyes, smiled, turned and walked away, though I thought to myself, *I may not have a snowball's chance in hell of winning our fight, but I just won this encounter.*

I kept asking Lou how he thought my chances would be fighting Reggie? All he said was, "Don't worry about it, you'll be all right."

It was finally April 27, 1979; and I was at The Robert Treat Hotel in Newark, New Jersey, for my first professional title fight. Lou reserved a hotel room for me so I could rest prior to the fight. After we got settled in, my good friend Jeff Simone and I walked around the hotel for a while. While I was on the elevator, a guy dressed in a chef's outfit holding a big round tray got on with us and said, "Penthouse, please."

On the way up, I asked this chef, "What's going on in the penthouse this evening?"

"Reggie Jones is defending his New Jersey Middleweight State Title tonight," he said. "He rented the penthouse; and, after he knocks out this chump he's fighting, he's throwing a big victory party. Once he puts this chump out of his misery, he'll fight for the World Middleweight Championship."

"Wish Reggie luck for me, he's going to need it," I told him.

"Why do you say that?"

"Because I'm the chump he has to knock out," I responded, "and he's in for the fight of his life."

Just as I said that, the elevator reached the top floor of the hotel, the penthouse. As the chef left, I told him, "Maybe I'll need your services after the fight."

Without saying a word, he just nodded his head and walked off the elevator

Featured as the main event, mine was the last fight of the evening. While Jeff and I wandered around the hotel waiting for my turn to fight, we paid a visit to the locker room for the other fighters on the show.

One of the fighters on the under-card was, from head to toe, a true born-and-raised Texan. He definitely looked like a man from Texas—big and strong with a true cowboy's accent. This night, he let his nerves get the best of him. He asked me how he should fight his opponent. I told him to go out and fight like he knew how to fight.

"You'll knock the other guy out quick."

Randal "Tex" Cob did exactly as I advised him, and he knocked out his opponent in the first round. Good job, Tex!

In my hotel room prior to the fight, I remember lying on my stomach, eyes closed, face down in a pillow. Worried? Yes, I was! I didn't know if I could fight for the entire twelve rounds. While lying there, I envisioned Reggie throwing punches at me. I would actually move my entire head and body to evade the imaginary punches. Hours went by, but it seemed like minutes. Then, it was time to go fight. I got up out of bed, put on my protective cup, boxing trunks, socks and boxing shoes.

I had never received a cut up to that point in my boxing career. In my corner for all of my pro fights was Lou's right-hand man, Ace Morrotta. He became known as one of the best cut men in the business. A cut man not only takes care of a fighter when he's cut during a fight, he also tapes the fighter's hands before the fight, gives the fighter water between each round, applies an ice bag on his face and always supplies moral support. Everyone who knew Ace carried the same opinion about him—friendly, and a nice person, always having a good encouraging word.

He taped my hands, first with layers of gauze, then white athletic tape. He wrapped my hands with this combination so well I could almost punch a brick wall without damaging my hand. I put the gloves on and straightened my fingers then Ace worked all the padding from the front of the glove backward towards my wrist with his fingers and put athletic tape around the bunched-up padding. With that accomplished, I made a fist, leaving my knuckles covered by only a thin layer of leather from the gloves. I hit myself a couple of times to see what it felt like. Oh, my God, it hurt!

I said to myself that Reggie's people were going to use the same tactics as Ace. That meant I was going to be hit with the same kind of unprotected knuckles. A scary thought for a second, before my attention switched over to warming up. It was time to leave the safety of my hotel room and go down to the arena to fight.

When we got off the elevator, with the ring in sight, the cheers of the crowd echoed in my ear. I remember Lou asking Chickie, "What kind of shape can I expect him to be in for this fight?"

"He's been training hard for the last month," Chickie said. "He should be in good enough shape."

I felt all eyes on me as I walked down the aisle. Finally, I was at the ring. I crawled up the steps, with applause from the fight fans. I started dancing around to get the feel of the padding on the ring floor and loosen up.

Reggie Jones always came in the ring last and made an impressive entrance, with rap music that he personally chose playing loudly over the P.A. system. He crawled through the ropes wearing a white satin robe with thin red and blue stripes around the wrists. There were similar stripes at the bottom of his boxing trunks. He moved around the ring with his arms raised over his head and threw some punches, warming up and looking very cocky. His trainer signaled for him to come over to his corner to take off his robe, displaying his New Jersey State Middleweight Championship Belt.

How beautiful, I thought. *I've never seen one up close and personal. Very impressive!* But it wasn't just the belt—it was what it stood for, and what it took to get it. I wanted that belt.

The fight began. The first two rounds went by quickly, with me controlling the pace. I followed my pre-fight strategy, and things were going well. I out-boxed him with my speed of foot, hit him with combinations and bounced back on my toes, constantly moving.

Then, midway through the third round, I lost my concentration for a moment. He pinned me on the ropes; and he felt strong, with a good center of gravity. Here came his big left hook, his best weapon. It caught me high on the right side of my head and buckled my knees. I remember the punch and its effects on me at the time. I leaned back into the ropes with my hands held high around the sides of my head for protection. Attempting to clear my head in a split second, I thought, *Does it end here?*

I think back to my amateur bout with Middleweight Champ Tommy Sullivan, when my heart failed me. I quit. When the referee asked me if I wanted to continue, I said *"No!"* There was no way that I would be quitting this time!

Reggie threw another left hook at me. I slipped it, tied him up and spun out off the ropes. Now, it was my turn. I hit him with a three-piece, with the left hook doing most of the damage. This proved to be a big turning point for me in the fight.

I come back by landing a hook-right hand combination, with force. For the first time in the fight, Reggie started to backpedal. From that point on, I dictated the pace. My foot feints totally faked him out: he threw punches at thin air, like swatting at flies. I threw punches fast, hard and accurately. When we fought inside, my right uppercut worked like a well-oiled chin-lifting machine.

Concentrating on the fight and losing track of the rounds already in the bag, I came back to the corner between rounds and asked Chickie, "What round am I in?"

"You're going into the tenth."

I could not believe it—the tenth round, and I was still there, not tired and doing well. That put a little bit of extra energy inside me. I said to myself, *I'm going to make it. I know I can finish the fight.*

In the twelfth round, as the fight was coming to an end, I threw a perfect lead right uppercut, landing squarely on his chin, buckling his knees and twisting his head around like Linda Blair in *The Exorcist*. Talk about timing! A split second later, the bell rang, ending the fight.

The crowd went crazy! People started climbing in the ring, running over to me, raising my hand over my head and lifting me up, yelling, "You did it, you did it." The ring announcer prepared to read the judges' results, and the referee signaled us to the center of the ring. I reached over, shook Reggie's hand and told him, "Good fight."

The announcer read the scores.

"Judge Phil Newman scores the fight 8-3-1 even, for Rosenberger."

A nice round of applause ensued, showing the crowd's approval.

He then read, "The referee Tony Perez scores the fight 5-5-2 rounds even, a draw."

The audience immediately booed his marks in disapproval.

With great anticipation, the announcer read off the third judge's score.

"Judge Harold Letterman scores the fight 9-3, for the

new New Jersey Middleweight State Champ, Rusty Rosenberger."

I started jumping up in the air with joy, yelling loud as I could, "I did it! I did it! I'm the champ! *Oh, my God*, I'm the champ!"

Lou congratulated me with a forced smile; I could tell he didn't mean it. Something bothered him; but at the time I didn't really care, nor did I concern myself with it. I had just pulled off a big upset, and no one and nothing was going to ruin that moment for me. That belt was mine!

When I woke up the next day, I sported a pair of black eyes. Reggie's best weapon ended up being the top of his head. Every time we ended up fighting in close, he ran the top of his head directly into my eyes.

Reggie turned out to be a real pro at using his head as a part of his offensive arsenal. In the clinches, my head kept popping up as to say "hi" to everyone—only it didn't come from an uppercut, but the top of his head hitting me in my face. I'm fortunate that my eyes didn't receive a cut from the numerous intentional head butts I got in those twelve rounds of boxing.

Three different boxing magazine reporters had come to write a story on Reggie, since they thought he would be fighting for the world title after he beat me—so they had thought. Now, the three reporters wanted to do an in-depth story on my short but outstanding boxing career and do a photo shoot. They asked the best way to get in touch with me. Being under the impression that a manager took care of his fighter's publicity, I gave the reporters Lou's name and phone number.

I received national coverage from one boxing magazine called *Boxing World* in their July-August edition in 1979. It shows a picture of Reggie and me fighting. I was throwing a right hand at Reggie as he bent over to avoid being hit by the punch. The article on the fight said "...Rusty got off strong and continued to have the upper hand for the remainder of the battle. Instead of tiring, as some thought he would, Rosenberger actually became stronger—and it was this that earned him the verdict...He went the twelve rounds in great style, and fought hard to win the title."

Earlier, I had received the honor of being voted prospect of the month by *Ring Magazine* in the April 1979 edition.

Promoters from our neighboring country of Canada also came to watch Reggie, hoping for a possible match-up between Reggie and Canadian Middleweight Champ Eddie Mello. Since I upset the apple cart, the promoters looked towards me for their future promotions.

How did I get to this pinnacle? Let me tell you about the road that took me there.

CHAPTER TWO

EARLY YEARS

It has always been my destiny to be a championship boxer. This destiny called to me from my younger years and will be with me as long as I live. This story is about that destiny, and what happened during my rise to the World Middleweight Championship and what I have been doing since.

I was raised with a competitive spirit by my father, Ray, a self-proclaimed fitness enthusiast who was a very intimidating figure, especially when he became angry. He had a set of eyes that could stare a hole right through you as he curled his upper lip tight against his top row of teeth, revealing his off-centered gold tooth.

Dad encouraged my younger brother and me to compete against each other physically for as long as I can remember. We called my brother Ray-Ray; then, after we started boxing, my dad nicknamed him "Razor." He was built well, a smaller version of me. We always argued and fought growing up, competing with each other in every sense of the word.

One day, meeting up in the basement, we had a slap fight. We had many of these—usually, I won. This time was different, though. This time, my brother held his hands up like the boxers I had seen on TV. He moved around on his toes like a ballerina and proceeded to slap me silly.

"Where did you learn to fight like that?" I asked him, after receiving a royal face whooping.

"Mr. Zippay, a schoolteacher, gives lessons at the YMCA," my brother said, "and he's looking for kids to train to fight in the Youngstown Golden Gloves."

The next day I waited at the front door of the YMCA for Mr. Zippay to show up. I wanted to be taught what my brother already knew. September of 1973 was the first time I ever trained in the art of boxing; I had just turned eighteen.

Mr. Zippay was a great guy who knew how to teach you the basics, and that was it. What I remember the most about Mr. Zippay were the words "la pancia." He told me it's Italian for "stomach." He'd tell me if I heard him say "la pancia" as I fought, that meant go to the body. I trained with him for a couple of months, and I still remember the first time I ever sparred against someone.

I fought a big black guy, a heavyweight by the name of Milton Poole. He had fought for a couple years already and knew a lot more about boxing than I did. When he hit me with a hard right hand, right on the button, I instantly saw a big white dot in my eyes, like someone had taken a picture with a flashbulb two feet from my face.

From that moment on, my destiny to be a fighter came alive in me. Taking that punch changed me. I became super-intense, and I started punching and didn't stop until Poole ended up sitting on the mat from what Mr. Zippay called "a vicious right hand." I didn't remember too much about it. It just happened. That's how it all started.

As I entered the world of boxing, I gathered as much information as I could. I was told about another guy who was a better trainer than Mr. Zippay. I thought, *If I'm going to do this, I might as well learn from the best I can find.*

In 1974, I started training with a World War II Army Boxing Champion by the name of Tony Mairiano from Girard, Ohio. He had trained fighters and been involved with the Golden Gloves for years. I soon found out that he knew the ropes better than Mr. Zippay did. Tony taught me how to be aggressive and how to use my natural body strength and punching power. He got me into great shape, and I entered the Youngstown Golden Gloves Tournament in 1974 in the middleweight division.

The tournament ran for three consecutive weeks. It was set up as single-loss elimination: lose one fight and you're out. The third week was always reserved for the finals, the championships.

In the first week, I received a *bye*—the right to proceed to the next round of competition without contesting the first one. The second week of the tournament was when I had my first fight. I fought against a guy who had experience on me—this was his second year fighting in the Golden Gloves. I hit him with a hard right hand, which left him bleeding badly from a cut over his left eye. My punching power, hand speed and physical conditioning proved too much for him. The referee stopped the fight in the third round on a TKO.

With that win, I qualified to fight in the finals. I was matched against a guy who had fought in both previous weeks of action, scoring two first-round KO's, a Puerto-Rican by the name of Louis Cruz who had once weighed over 200 pounds but lost weight—a bunch of weight. Tall and hard-punching, he wore a long ponytail held with a rubber band. With his two first-round KOs, he was the favorite to win the Golden Gloves that year in the Novice Middleweight Division.

The novice division is for fighters who have had five fights or fewer, or haven't won a championship. The open division is for any fighter with five or more fights under their belt, or who has won a Golden Gloves Championship.

The night before my first-ever championship boxing match, my father and I were playing ping-pong in the basement of our home. As we played, my father stopped for a moment, looked me in my eyes and said, "This Cruz guy you're fighting tomorrow night is tough—maybe you should think about dropping out."

I said to him, "Cruz may be tough and can punch hard and has knocked out all his opponents so far, but he's never fought anyone like me. If it's the last thing I do, Dad, I'm going to knock out his ponytail."

The night of the Golden Gloves finals was February 6, 1974. The Golden Gloves was always held at the Struthers Field House in Struthers, a suburb of Youngstown, Ohio. The arena was packed with a lot of fans who were making a whole lot of noise, and I was nervous. When it came my turn to fight, as I crawled into the ring and through the ropes, I looked across to get a glimpse of my opponent. There he stood, with a cocky, confident look in his eyes, ready to knock me out or do bodily harm to me, if I let him.

The bell rang, starting this contest of strength, courage and boxing ability. I really don't remember much after he hit me with that first hard right hand. I saw that flash again, and the next thing I knew the referee was raising my hand in victory. I won on a TKO in the second round. I had just won my first-ever boxing championship.

As I stood there looking at Cruz, I took a quick inventory on the effects my punches had had on him. I had broken his nose, cut him over his right eye; and, yes, I knocked that ponytail completely out of its rubber band. Though I had taken a few punches to my facial area in the course of this match, my skin remained intact—no cuts or bruises. I'm glad I didn't take my father's advice.

The icing on the cake came when the Golden Gloves

officials presented me with the "Most Outstanding Fighter of the Tournament" trophy.

* * *

Niles Boxer Takes Gloves Title

By Ron Ceretelli
Times *Sports Writer*

Middleweight Rusty Rosenberger showed why he earned the special award with the first TKO of the evening at the expense of Louis Cruz. Rosenberger bloodied Cruz's nose scoring with rights. When a left-right combination landed solidly, the referee stopped the fight on the advice of the ringside doctor with only 40 seconds gone into the third round. Rosenberger was named the "Most Promising of the Tournament" and received a trophy.

Niles boxing fans took special interest in the 1974 Golden Gloves tournament. That interest was Rusty Rosenberger, who won the 1974 Most Promising Novice Award in the 160-pound division. Rusty earned his trophy by winning his first fight in a three-round decision and advanced to the finals, where he registered a TKO over favored Louis Cruz with only 40 seconds gone into the third round.

Rusty, a 1973 graduate of Niles McKinley High School, began his boxing career under the instruction of Dan Zippay at the Niles YMCA. Rusty follows a rigorous training schedule set up by his trainer Tony Maiorana, a boxing figure whose fighting experience dates back to before WWII. Rusty is currently enrolled at Youngstown State University where he is majoring in Business Management.

CHAPTER THREE

LEARNING

Shortly thereafter, I met a fellow by the name of Bob Miketa. He told me that he watched me fight in the Gloves a couple months before. He said, "You impressed me with your punching power, hand speed and conditioning."

Then he told me something that stuck in my head for the remainder of my career. He said, "If you knew how to move your feet as well as you moved your hands, you could be a real champ."

At first, I didn't comprehend what he meant. Following my workouts in the gym and once I got home, I collected some fight films of great fighters from the past and present, my favorite being the greatest boxer of all time, Muhammad Ali. After Mom fed me dinner, I'd go to the basement and watch fight films on the old Super 8 projector.

The fights I watched always inspired me, motivated me to hit my heavy bag and speed bag for a few rounds—which is what I did next—each and every night. Oftentimes, I'd go for a short run afterward; I love to run.

My parents owned a beautiful ranch-style brick home,

located right next to Waddell Park in Niles, Ohio. The park contained baseball fields, a football field, an ice-skating pond, about two acres of land with lots of shade trees, picnic tables, charcoal grills and a big municipal swimming pool that our backyard ran right into. I really enjoyed running along the park roads.

Bob Miketa impressed me with his knowledge of how a fighter should move on his feet. He educated me on how valuable foot movement is for a boxer. He taught me how to throw foot feints—that's where you move your body forward like you are going to throw a punch, only you stop short of entering your opponent's punching or contact zone. Your opponent will actually think you're moving into his punching range. If your foot feints are quick and sharp enough, your opponent will react by throwing a punch in defense. He'll completely miss you while making himself look out-of-control. Once he commits to your foot feints and he extends his arm trying to hit you, he gives you the perfect opportunity to react with a counterpunch over his extended arm.

It took a few weeks of practice in the gym, working on the footwork and with hand pads/focus mitts to get my timing down to perfection. Once I accomplished that, I put it into practice during sparring sessions. I mean I started banging my sparring partners with some mean right-hand counters over their extended left jabs. They didn't even know what hit them, or where it came from.

It's the same exact technique that Ali used to knock out Sonny Liston. You know, the "phantom punch," the second time they fought. It came out of nowhere—so fast that, to this day, some critics say Liston took a fall.

If you ever have the chance to view that fight, watch. When it comes time and Ali hits him with the so-called "phantom punch," put your VCR on slow motion and study Ali's feet and right hand. What you'll see is Liston throwing a hard left jab at Ali. Ali steps back with his right foot, just enough to make Liston's jab fall short of his face. As Liston is pulling his jab back, Ali launches a quick, hard, devastating right hand right over his extended left jab, all this accomplished in a fraction of a second. Ali's punch is pinpoint accurate to Liston's unsuspecting chin.

I practiced this technique that Bob and Ali taught me over and over again. Before too long, it became second nature to me. It became a reaction, instead of something I had to think about. I developed the punch to be fast, accurate and powerful.

Because of our intense rivalry growing up, no one went to the gym more than my brother and I. My brother helped me the most in fine-tuning my foot feints, counter right hands and overall boxing skills—and I helped him, too.

Although my brother weighed twenty pounds less than I did, he fought me harder than anyone I ever came up against. I think it's called "sibling rivalry." He had extremely fast hands, a hard left hook and a burning desire to never let me get the best of him. People came off the streets just to watch us spar with each other, saying that it was something worth paying to see.

But our rivalry didn't mean that my brother and I disliked each other—far from it. I remember preparing for a fight on a Saturday, and no one showed up at the gym for me to spar with.

Bob asked me, "What's Razor doing today? Give him a call and see if he'll come to the gym to give you some work."

I called, and my brother agreed to come to help me. The gym was located on top of a club named the R-B Club, located in Warren, Ohio, on Route 422, a bar and nightclub-type establishment. Bob and I worked out on the hand pads/focus mitts until I heard a car's horn beep.

When I heard my brother's horn, I jumped out of the

ring and ran to the front door to let him in. As I looked out into the parking lot, I saw Razor's car butted up against another car; and Razor and this big guy were arguing.

I walked out and asked him, "What's the problem?"

Razor says, "This mother f----er ran into the back of my car." As soon as he said that, the big guy started chasing him. I immediately threw off my boxing gloves and ran down the steps to meet this guy head-on. They ran around the back of the car, first Razor and then the big guy in hot pursuit. I met this big guy—or I should say my right hand met this big guy's face. Down he went.

As he attempted to get up, I grabbed hold of his belt with one hand and the back his shirt collar with the other hand and ran his head into the side of the building. Down and out for the count—the count of about two hundred-fifty, that is.

Later, the guy came up to Razor and me and apologized. He blamed it on one too many beers. If he was on his way to being drunk at eleven in the morning, then I guess he got what he deserved.

In the ring sparring, I hit Razor with a powerful right hand; he took it as he usually did. The bell rang, ending the second round. He walked back to his corner, stopped and turned around.

"Well, I guess you won that round," he told me.

"What do you mean?" I asked him.

He smiled at me, revealing his front teeth. His top front tooth was missing.

"What happened?" I asked him.

"You know that last right hand you hit me with? I forgot my mouthpiece today, and you broke my tooth in half."

You can tell who my dad favored, between my brother and me: he nicknamed me "Rusty" and my brother "Razor."

The only thing that held Razor back from becoming a

great boxer was his lack of discipline. Every morning, I'd get up at six o'clock to do my roadwork. Razor liked to stay out until three in the morning, partying and drinking. I can't tell you how many times we almost got into fights with each other because I woke him up and tried to encourage him to get up and go running with me.

CHAPTER FOUR

A NEW OUTLOOK

I'd been training with Miketa for about two weeks when he booked me a fight. I was going to fight a bad kid, bad in two ways. He'd spent most of his childhood in a reformatory school for unruly children. While in this reformatory, he entered a boxing program for these problem kids. He ended up becoming the middleweight champ of this school—real tough and undefeated.

I was still learning how to fight, slowly but surely catching on, showing and feeling improvement. The kid looked in real good shape, threw lots of punches; but my conditioning, body strength, punching power and determination won me a close decision.

His camp protested.

"We'll gladly give you a rematch," Miketa told them. With that promise made, we all shook hands and went back to that proverbial blackboard.

Scheduled one month to the day after our original match, the fight was going to be tough; and I knew it. Bob and I worked on my footwork and another important aspect of being a successful boxer—the know-how and ability to slip punches. We worked hard and long every day leading up to the fight.

The show was held in the basement of a bar in Bakerstown, PA. The ring was set up on the basement floor, with very little padding underfoot. If I stood in the middle of the ring and raised my hand up over my head, I touched the ceiling.

I got into the ring and looked across to my opponent's corner. He returned a glare. The referee finished giving us the pre-fight instructions in the middle of the ring. I extended my gloved hand to touch his in a sportsman-like fashion.

"Let's fight," he said. He turned and went back to his corner.

The bell rang. We met in the center of the ring, he threw a left jab and I stepped back from the on-coming punch and danced away. He followed me in and repeated the same punch. This time I stayed in close and slipped it—I avoided it by bending my knees slightly, tilting my head to the right just enough to let the punch go by. I then danced back out of range.

When he attempted to throw his third consecutive jab at me, I slipped in the same fashion and countered over top of his jab with the "Phantom Punch." In that small room, the entire crowd saw, heard and reacted to the punch with a roar.

That set the stage and tempo for the rest of the fight. My power kept him pinned on the ropes, absorbing a lot of hard, accurate bombs for most of the first round. During that round, the referee gave him two standing eight counts. I was moving in for the kill when the bell rang, ending the first round of action.

At the start of the second round, he tried to take control by tying me up and pushing me back into a corner. The referee stepped in and separated us. I circled out to my left, threw a quick, deceptive foot feint and had him swatting at the air. I then stepped in with a jab-right hand combination that landed right on his chin, buckling his knees. The referee stepped in and gave him another standing eight count.

As action resumed, I threw a lead left hook and a straight right hand combination, both punches landing with devastating power on his chin, sending him literally flying through the ropes out of the ring onto the bare concrete floor. The referee wisely stopped the fight, raising my hand in victory via a second-round KO.

After the fight and the cheering crowd settled down, the officials presented me with a trophy for the "Most Outstanding Fighter;" and I received a standing ovation from the audience for my domination of the fight. He did tag me a couple good punches to my facial area, but I received no cuts or bruises. My face was still unmarked.

I lived a half-hour drive from Youngstown, Ohio, and traveled there often to get sparring at some of the boxing gyms in the city. We trained at the Buckeye Elks on the north side, with Pedro Tomez the head trainer, and at another gym called the Methodist Community Center on the east side of Youngstown, run by a man named Will Brandon.

With my punching power, fast reflexes, great stamina and improving overall boxing skills, I had trouble finding sparring partners. The ones I could count on with any regularity were three heavyweights and my brother.

When we traveled to the Methodist Community Center for a workout, I always sparred with a heavyweight named Amos Haynes. He stood 6 feet, 4 inches and weighed two hundred-fifteen pounds. During one of our sparring matches, Amos threw a left jab at me; and, with perfect coordination and timing, I hit him with the phantom punch. Down he went to pay a brief visit to the canvas.

He was a big, strong man who could fight in the gym like a real champ. We fought many a war, many tough workouts. I knew he could fight, but something inside him just wouldn't let it come out. When he got in front of a crowd of people, he always froze up. I would get really upset when I watched him fight.

"Punch, Amos, punch, man. Come on! You're in shape! Fight, man, fight!" I'd yell at him from ringside.

He was obviously a better athlete than most of his opponents, but he would just stand there and take a beating. It never made any sense to me. Just to give you an idea of the athletic ability he possessed…

The year was 1975; and before our training session I asked him if he could dunk a basketball. He smiled, revealing his shiny, bright gold front tooth and said, "Are you kidding?"

"No, I'm not kidding, can you?" I said.

At the center, the boxing gym was located in the basement. Upstairs was a basketball court. After our workout he took me up the stairs to the basketball court, picked up a basketball and said, "Watch this."

He dribbled to center court, stood there briefly and then dribbled and ran towards one of the hoops. When he reached the foul line, he jumped in the air and spun. As he spun in the air, he slam-dunked the ball over and behind his head. Man, did that impress me.

Afterward, I asked him," Can you do that with a crowd of people watching you?"

"With no problem whatsoever," he told me.

I then asked him, "Why can't you fight the way you can play basketball in front of a crowd of people?"

All he did was lower his head and said, "I don't know."

He could have been a great one.

I also trained with another heavyweight named Terry Nicopolis. He weighed around three hundred-fifty pounds. For a man his size, he could really fight. He threw his punches quick and powerful and owned a deadly left hook.

This one time—and only this one time—as he tried to decapitate me with his left hook I stepped inside of the oncoming punch and hit him with one of my own. In a flash he went down—and just as fast was back up ready to go.

Another heavyweight who helped sharpen my skills was Phil Brozier. He didn't punch all that hard, but he could fight. He threw a lot of nice combinations and had the ability to slip punches and a chin like a rock. I've hit him with punches that could have knocked out a bull, and he took them all and kept coming.

He would lead with his head, and on many occasions his head hit me in the eyes. He and I sparred hundreds of rounds during the years we trained together; and, though he did hit me with them many, many times, I never received a cut from his frequent, unintentional head-butts.

On two different occasions, I knocked down two different heavyweights. On both occasions, afterwards in the locker room talking, each one told me the same thing—the only time someone had hit them harder was when they sparred with Ernie Shavers, boxing's hardest-punching heavyweight to date.

Ernie Shavers trained at the same gym, the Warren AC on Nevada Street in Warren, Ohio. You talk about a big, strong, powerful man! This guy could punch like no one I've ever seen. I watched his manager, Blacky Genero, bring him in sparring partners from New York City, Philadelphia and Chicago; and he just busted them up. None of the sparring partners lasted more than a couple days.

I watched Ernie tear into these fighters with intent to literally take their heads right off their shoulders; and, many times, he almost did. One day, he asked me to spar with him. With visions fresh in my mind of his demolition of those poor sparring partners, I, without hesitation, answered him, *"No, thanks."*

CHAPTER FIVE

AMATEUR DAYS

Early in my boxing career, I attended a fight show to watch a fighter by the name of Darrell Frazier. He fought very impressively—the way he moved on his feet, his boxing skills and his overall performance. I went to the locker room afterwards to congratulate him and praise him on his outstanding fight.

I told him, "In the future, I hope I can become as accomplished a fighter in the ring as you."

He smiled and said, "Keep training and working hard, you can do it."

Almost before I knew it, it was time to start training for the 1975 Golden Gloves Tournament. My weight at the time was one hundred sixty-five pounds. In 1975, the middleweight limit was one hundred-sixty pounds. I really didn't have an extra five pounds to lose, already being in great shape, hard as a rock, with not an ounce of fat anywhere to be found on my physique.

So, rather than lose that extra five pounds to make the middleweight division, I entered the light heavyweight division, where the maximum weight is one hundred seventy-five pounds. I figured it would be better if I didn't make myself weak by losing that additional five pounds of muscle.

Only four fighters were entered in the light heavyweight division in the year of 1975. We all received a bye the first week of competition, and were scheduled to fight in the second week. I was matched up against a strong, experienced fighter by the name of Joey Sallerino. Because of his past fighting experience, he automatically became a slight favorite to win.

I proved to be too much for this guy, whom I beat badly. He bled from his nose and from a nasty gash over his left eye. The referee mercifully stopped it in the third round.

That put me in line to fight Darrell Frazier, the defending champ for the past two years. I had some concern because of his boxing skills and experience.

* * *

I trained hard for this championship fight. I can remember my girlfriend's father, Mickey, stopping by the gym to watch me train. I was working out on the hand pads/focus mitts with my trainer, Bob Miketa, until the bell rang ending the round.

"Man, you look tough," he said. "You're punching hard and fast. You're ready, that's for sure."

The night of the finals for the Youngstown Golden Gloves Championships was February 15, 1975. The novice fighters always fought first, which meant that I had a long wait until I was on center stage.

I walked around the Struthers Field House for what seemed like hours. The field house was packed—not an empty seat in the place, standing room only.

I walked by the dressing room, and Bob told me it was time to get my hands wrapped. From the time he wrapped my hands until time to fight seemed like a second. My stomach felt like someone let a thousand butterflies loose in it. Bob put the gloves on, raised his hands and proceeded to warm me up by having me throw punches on his bare hands.

Bob and I had trained long and hard for this, our first championship fight together. He told me over and over again, "Put your punches together and move."

After the introductions, I walked back to my corner. Bob and Chuck were both waiting for me, to slap me five and wish me luck. The bell rang, I danced out of my corner and the first combination I threw was a left hook, right hand. Thinking I'd missed him with both punches, I looked down on the canvas. There my opponent lay. For the longest time, he didn't move. I had just KO'd the defending champ in the first round.

The ring announcer made the trophy presentation to me and announced my name "the new Youngstown Golden Gloves Open Division Light heavyweight Champ." He didn't stop, but continued by saying that, "This KO will be recorded as the fastest KO in the history of the Youngstown Golden Gloves in the open division during a championship fight, thirty-eight seconds of the first round."

* * *

Rosenberger Scores TKO
By Dick Olmstead
Tribune *Sports Writer*

Struthers—Rusty Rosenberger came out of his corner at the opening bell with fist flailing to once again salvage what had turned out to be a bad night for Niles area boxers in the Golden Gloves Tournament finals last night.

Rosenberger was pitted against the 1974 defending champ in the 175 lb. open-division, Darnell Frazier. With only 38 seconds after the bout began, the Niles Bomber was the new champ, as Frazier never even had time to land a punch.

* * *

The Cleveland Golden Gloves Regional Tournament was the next one to set my sights on. While I was standing in line waiting to get weighed in, I heard the weigh-in official say, "Dokes, 175."

That caused my heart to skip a beat—more like two. In my mind and my heart, I didn't think I weighed the same as Mike Dokes. I thought he fought heavyweight. I had seen him fight on national TV twice.

With my confidence level plummeting, the weigh-in official says, "Rosenberger, 165." He looks at me and says, "Man, you're only 165 pounds, and you're fighting in the light heavyweight division? You're going to get yourself hurt if you're not careful, especially if you have to fight Mike Dokes."

I pulled out of that tournament and headed back to Niles with my tail between my legs. I did go the finals of the 1975 Cleveland Golden Gloves, Mike Dokes vs. Pablo Ramos for the championship. Dokes won a close decision.

I went back to the gym, training every day, waiting for the next smoker to come up. A *smoker* is the name given to fight shows promoted by people who enjoyed boxing and enjoyed making money by promoting boxing shows—not a tournament, but fights held one night and one night only.

The two guys who ran the gym I worked out in, Moe and Jimmy, planned on putting on a smoker. They wanted me to be the main event. I gladly agreed. They matched me up to fight a guy by the name of Mel "Tiger" Brown, from Weirton, W.Va. The show was held in Warren, Ohio, at the Packard Music Hall, on May 16, 1975.

As I got out of my car at the Packard Music Hall, I was met by two reporters, one from the *Warren Tribune*, Larry Wringler, and, from the *Niles Times*, Sal Marino. They asked my thoughts about the upcoming fight—what I thought about my opponent.

I told them, "I've never heard of or seen this guy fight before, so I really didn't know what to expect." I also told them, "I'm in good shape. Bob's been working with me, getting me sharp; and I'm ready for anything he, (Tiger) brings to the ring."

I walked into the dressing room where they had set up the scale to conduct the weigh-ins. I walked through the door and saw a black guy sitting on a chair, all sprawled out, lying back with his legs extended out as far as possible. As I walked by him, he said to me, "Are you Rosenberg?"

"Yes, I am, why?" I said.

"They sure fucked you up tonight, boy," he responded.

"Why do you say that?" I asked.

"'Cause you're fighting me, and I'm going to knock you out."

"You want to get it on right now?" I asked him.

He jumped up out of the chair, grabbed me by my shirt, pulled me towards him and put me in a bear hug. I twisted and turned until I broke free from his grasp, ready to throw a punch at him. By this time Bob and his trainer stepped in and separated us from each other.

He made a big mistake acting that way. By fight time, I was burning mad—ready to go to war. The bell sounded; and I flew across the ring, hitting him on the chin with an infuriated right hand. He dropped to the canvas like someone had cut off his legs.

After receiving a standing eight count, Tiger immediately grabbed me and tied me up. I remember seeing him spit out his mouthpiece and wondering why. The next thing I knew, I felt a sharp pain in my chest. I looked down and saw Tiger's teeth sinking into my skin. He was biting me!

I tried to keep my composure and stay focused. I hit him again and again, dropping him for a second time. After the eight count, he repeated the biting again.

It turned into a free-for-all. I kept fighting, and every time we got in a clinch he bit me. When the referee finally stopped the fight in the middle of the second round, the crowd was going crazy; and I was bleeding from seven different bite marks.

The fans started booing, throwing cups, papers, programs, anything they could get their hands on, into the ring. If more Afro-Americans had come to watch, there probably would have been a riot. If not for the fast response of the city of Warren, Ohio's, finest, who knows?

After a short period of time, the officials awarded me the win on a disqualification. I paid a visit to the Trumbull Memorial Hospital following the fight to get a tetanus shot, just in case. Now we know why they nicknamed him "Tiger."

* * *

Brawl Mars Warren AC Boxing Program
By Larry Ringler
Tribune *Sports*

Warren—Rusty Rosenberger hooked up in a bloody, reckless match against Mel "Tiger" Brown. The fight was stopped in the second round. According to many eyewitnesses, it was reported they saw Brown actually biting Rosenberger. It also was reported that there were five visual bleeding bite marks on Rosenberger's chest and shoulder areas.

CHAPTER 6

HEART FAILURE

The year was 1976. In just two years, my boxing skills had developed. I was someone to be taken seriously, especially if you fought me. At twenty-one years old, I could end a fight with one punch and had great footwork and a burning desire to become the best the world had ever seen. I didn't want to do anything else. I wanted to be the best, the World Middleweight Champ; and I was willing to commit everything I had to my boxing career. I wanted it that bad.

While chasing my dream, my destiny, I had to work. My father had run his own a small business since 1961. He owned and operated a home-interior remodeling store. He sold carpeting, linoleum, ceramic tile and wallpaper, and had two crews of men to install for him. I worked for him from the time my mother made me quit college in 1974 to go to work with him—she wanted me to keep an eye on him—until I moved to New Jersey to pursue my boxing destiny in 1978.

Dad was one of the greatest, if not *the* greatest, womanizers ever. He was a very handsome man, with a bodybuilder's physique, huge powerful hands and an off-centered gold front tooth he got in the Navy during WWII that made his smile stand out like a lighthouse in the fog. Dad cheated on Mom so much that after thirty-eight years of less than wedded bliss, she finally divorced him.

Bob Miketa made connections in Pennsylvania and West Virginia and entered me in two tournaments, one in each of those states. One was the Silver Gloves in Weirton, W.Va., held at the Millsop Community Center. The other was the Diamond Belt Championship in Monroeville, Pa., held at the Monzo's Howard Johnson's just outside of Pittsburgh.

When I fought in Monroeville, I had two matches in consecutive weeks. I scored a first-round KO and a second-round KO, respectively. After the championship match, I was on my way back to the dressing room. To get there, you had to ride the elevator up to the fifth floor. As fate would have it, the guy I had just KO'd and won the championship from got on the elevator the same time I did.

As we ascended to the fifth floor, Bob, who was still with me at the time, congratulated me on a job well done.

"You landed a lucky shot, and I'll kick your ass right here and now," the guy I had just fought said.

"The fight's over," I said. "Just leave it alone."

"I thought so," he said. "You're scared to fight outside of the ring."

"Man," I told him, "you want some of me, come get it."

With that, this guy took a step towards me and raised his fist as if he was about to hit me. I reacted with a beautiful straight right hand.

When we had fought in the ring a few minutes earlier, the referee had stopped the fight after the third time I knocked him down in the second round. This time when I hit him, his trainer and a friend carried him off the elevator.

The next tournament I entered was the one in Weirton, W.Va., at the Millsop Community Center. While I was standing in line waiting to be weighed in, from across the room, I heard, "Hey, Rosenberg, what are you doing on my turf?"

I looked through the crowd of fighters gathered in the locker room to find the owner of the voice that was calling me. As I did, lo and behold, it was Tiger Brown. We shook hands, smiled at each other and started talking. After only a couple minutes of talking, being a little leery of him from our previous encounter, I realized he wasn't as crazy as I thought he was.

During our conversation, I asked him why he bit me during our fight.

He said, "Man, Rosenberg, you punch so hard I didn't want to take no ass-kicking, I did what I had to do, but I apologize for my actions."

As Tiger and I talked, he told me of this Polish guy named Komininski who had entered the tournament.

"Man, Rosenberg, you don't want to fight him," Tiger said.

"Why?" I asked.

"Because this guy is an animal," he replied. "When I fought him last year I hit him with all my might and couldn't even slow him down, and he punches like a mule kicks. He's nuts."

As fate or my luck turned out, I drew Komininski to fight in the semifinals. The previous year's defending middleweight champ, Rick Noggle, was sitting ringside. He'd fought this Komininski the previous year and won a hard-fought, close, three-round split decision, from what Tiger told me.

The bell rang for the first round, and I tried to keep my distance and box him. He felt strong, and had a street fighter's mentality. He couldn't really box, but he could punch—hard. I controlled the first half of round one. Then, I guess I got lazy, or my mind drifted somewhere other than concentrating on the wild mountain man before me, who was literally trying to take my head off. All I really remember is seeing it coming and getting hit by his right hand, right on the chin and seeing a flash before my eyes. The next thing I remember, my hand was raised in victory.

Arriving back at my corner, I asked Bob, "What happened?"

"Yeah, like you don't know," he said with a laugh.

"For real, Bob," I said. "I don't know. What happened?"

"You knocked this tough mother out. Look, he's still laying on the mat."

I looked over in the direction of where a crowd of people were gathered. The kid's father, mother and some friends were standing at ringside crying, all these concerned people looking over his prone body lying in the ring. I walked over to check on the kid. As I came near, they remove an ice bag from his forehead, revealing a huge goose egg that was turning all red and blue in color.

They carried Komininski out of the ring and back to the locker room. He eventually woke up and got to his feet. He did hit me with a strong, hard right hand to my face, but I received no cuts or bruises. Thank *God* for that.

A week went by, and I found myself once again at the Millsop Community Center to fight for the Silver Belt Middleweight Championship. Bob and I entered the community center and waited for the scale to be set up. The promoter of the show, George Milner, told Bob that the defending champ, Rick Noggle, hadn't shown up yet. Because he was from Canton, Ohio, they could have got stuck in traffic or had a flat tire or got lost. The man told Bob not worry, though, and that they would be there.

I weighed in and went through my regular routine of walking around the arena during the first part of the show. That always helped to settle my nerves and loosen my muscles up. Bob started taping my hands when George approached us with some bad news—or good news, depends on how you look at it. George told us that Noggle had dropped out of the tournament. Something about a cut over his eye he received while sparring in preparation for his championship fight with me.

"Things happen for a reason," as the saying goes. I was awarded the 1976 Millsop Community Center Silver Gloves Middleweight Championship. I only fought one fight in this tournament and won the championship, but the officials of the show still awarded me with the "Most Outstanding Fighter of the Tournament" trophy.

Next, it was on to Youngstown and my third championship fight in as many years. In 1976, I fought a man by the name of Maurice Fleming, the 1974-1975 Youngstown Middleweight Champ. He fought out of the same gym as a sparring partner and friend of mine, Amos Haynes.

Amos and I talked on the team bus on our way to Cleveland to fight in the North-East Ohio Golden Gloves Championships. He told me later that, as he watched us fight, "Maurice chose to fight you with his hands positioned down at his waist. I told my friend he better get his hands up, 'cause Rosenberg punches hard."

He then said, "A split second later you hit him with a tremendous body shot which drove back into the ropes. When the ropes thrust him off, you hit him with a perfectly timed lead hook-straight right hand combination.

"After the referee helped Maurice up off the floor, he received a standing eight count. At the count of eight, the referee asked Maurice if he wanted to continue, and he said nodded his head. [Referee Joey Bishop] stood between you two, raised his hand in the air and yelled, 'box.'

"You stepped towards Maurice and hit him with a right hand-left hook, knocking him out of the ring, through the ropes onto the official's table ringside. At this point, the referee looked into Maurice's glassy eyes and wisely stopped the fight. I told my friend you could punch hard—now he believes me."

* * *

That win put me in line to fight in the Regional Golden Gloves Tournament in Cleveland, Ohio. The first night at the regionals, I was in the locker room. At least a hundred other boxers stood there, all waiting to be weighed in.

The first night of competition, I received a "bye." In the second week of action, I scored a first-round knockout over an older guy. What I mean by an older guy—if you're twenty-one or older, and he was, it automatically puts you into the open division. With only two fights under his belt, this guy didn't have any real experience in the ring, but he tried very hard to give me the best fight he could. That phantom right hand, though, did the trick quick.

That set me up to fight in the Cleveland Golden Gloves finals against Rick Noggle. Once again, I was standing in line waiting to be weighed in. Noggle approached me and asked me if I had ever had fought Maurice Fleming.

"Yes," I told him. "I fought him in the finals at the Youngstown Golden Gloves Tournament."

"I fought him last year in the Cleveland Golden Gloves Regional Championships," Noggle said.

"How did you do against him?" I asked.

"I beat him over a three-round decision," he replied. "How'd you do against him?"

When I told Noggle "I knocked him out in the first round," I almost had to get a car jack to pick up his mouth off the floor.

What I told him about the outcome of my title fight against Fleming, coupled with my first-round knock-out of Komininski in Weirton, shook his confidence. He knew I was going to give him a real fight, the fight for the Cleveland Golden Gloves Middleweight Championship.

The championship fight between Rick Noggle, the 1974-75 defending champ, and the new kid on the block, Rusty Rosenberger, was billed as the main event that night. The fight started out with that phantom right hand almost ripping Noggle's head right off his shoulders. What a right hand I hit him with, another perfect rendition of the phantom punch—a hard, quick, straight right hand over his extended left jab that shook his entire cranium.

To my surprise, it didn't knock him off his feet. Everyone else I'd hit with that punch had to be carried out of the ring. I looked to see what damage it had done to him. Unbelievably, he came right back, firing punches at me that backed me up into a corner.

I tied him up until the referee came in and separated us. It was than I realized that I was in a real fight myself. All the training and hard work I had gone through enabled me to keep my composure and stick to my fight plan, though—out-box him with speed of foot, hand speed, punching power and overall ring tactics.

The first round seemed close, but in the second round my punching power and body strength started to take their toll on him. I won the second round by a comfortable margin.

Going into the third and final round, I took control by landing some hard, devastating right hands and left hooks early. The entire third round he backpedaled or, I should say, ran. Talk about timing. I threw a hook and right hand with both punches landing cleanly on his chin. The right hand landed with a thud; and, a split second later, the bell rang, ending the fight.

The referee brought us to the center of the ring as the announcer read the judge's decision. He raised my hand in victory. I had won on all three judges' scorecards, winning the Cleveland Golden Gloves by a unanimous decision.

* * *

Rosenberger Wins AAU Boxing Berth

Warren Tribune
Saturday, March 13, 1976

Cleveland—Rusty Rosenberger, the smooth-working middleweight fighting for the Warren R-B Club under the direction of Bob Miketa and Chuck Nelson, fought his way into the national AAU boxing tournament with a convincing decision over defending champ from Canton, 165-pound Rick Noggle, in the finals of the Cleveland Golden Gloves Tournament here Friday night. Rosenberger, a Niles fighter in the Warren stable and a three-time champion in the Youngstown Golden Gloves Tournaments, advances to the Florida event the week of March 21, 1976. Other district champs who were upset were Jeff Stoudemire, 132, Cleveland, who dropped a split decision to Harry Arroyo of Youngstown, and Gary Pope, 147, Eastlake, who was decisively beaten by Art McKnight of Mansfield. The finals were enjoyed by a crowd of over 3,000 fight fans at the Lincoln-West High School.

* * *

I had now qualified to fight in the national Golden Gloves,

which would be held in Miami, Florida. The boxing show was being held right in the middle of the Orange Bowl.

I really trained hard for this, my first national competition. My mother took me out and bought me a new pink three-piece suit to wear when I flew to Miami. I was going in style.

Two weeks before I was scheduled to fly to Florida to fight in the nationals, I was shadow boxing in the basement of my home when a near-disaster struck. I was looking in the mirror, throwing punches into the air. It was fate, I guess. I threw a right hand with all the fury, speed and power that I threw my right hands with in the ring. I misjudged the distance to the edge of the door; my right hand pinkie knuckle hit the edge with a crash. I split my knuckle wide open.

For the next two weeks, all I could do to prepare for the nationals was shadow box, run and do my exercises. I almost pulled out, but when I thought of spending a week in the Florida sun with all expenses paid, I said, "Oh, well, I'll go and do my best."

I had befriended a fellow boxer on the Youngstown team who had won in the lightweight division, Harry Arroyo. He and I bonded on this trip. We roomed together, we ate together and we cheered each other on when we fought. He is a real nice guy and an exceptionally talented boxer.

My trainer, Bob, who had traveled to Miami with the team representing the Northeast Ohio region, found me poolside sunbathing the day before the nationals started. As he and I walked through the hotel, we saw a crowd of people huddled around this one black guy.

"Who's that guy, anyway?" I asked.

"I don't know. Let's go over and find out," Bob said.

So, we walked towards the crowd of people. As we got closer, we heard someone say, "That's Sugar Ray

Leonard."

I had heard about him from reading the newspaper, magazines and seeing him on TV. I walked right up to him, introduced myself and extended my hand, expecting a handshake. I not only got a handshake but a hug as well, and he told me, "I've heard your name. You won the Golden Gloves in Cleveland, right?"

He wished me luck, leaving me with the impression that he was a great fighter, a gentleman and a first-class human being.

After meeting Mr. Leonard, Bob told me he had picked up the line-up for the next day's fights. He wore a worried look on his face.

"What's up? What's wrong?" I asked him.

"You drew the 1975 National Golden Gloves Champ, Tommy Sullivan."

I hadn't sparred in two weeks! To be completely honest, I felt scared to death!

Then, it was fight time, and I was about to go on. The bell rang, and I wasn't moving like I normally do. Mr. Sullivan couldn't hit hard at all; but he was throwing punches, and I wasn't. In the second round, the referee stopped the fight because of my inactivity. My heart quit, and I quit.

* * *

Rosenberger Bows in Golden Gloves

Miami, Fla.—Rusty Rosenberger, the Warren area's lone standard bearer in the National Golden Gloves Tournament here, was stopped in the second round of his 165-pound class fight with defending champion and Pan American Games gold medalist Tom Sullivan of Las Vegas, Wednesday night.

* * *

I felt ashamed and embarrassed. I was not looking forward to going back home a real loser, at having to face all my fans, friends and all the young kids who had looked up to me. It would be hard to show my face around the hotel where all the other boxers stayed.

When I arrived at the hotel and had made it up to my room, Arroyo patiently waited. He, too, fought and lost on a decision. We were consoling each other when the phone rang. It was a good friend that had flown to Miami to watch me fight; his name, Mike Javorniky.

"I met Angelo Dundee and told him all about you," Mike said. "As a matter of fact, I gave him your phone number. He said he'd like to talk to you. He said he seen you fight last night and remembers you and liked what he saw."

I replied, "Yeah, right. If he said that, I don't know why. What could he see and like in a quitter?"

About a half-hour later, the phone rang again. I answered it. On the other end was a guy claiming to be Angelo Dundee.

"Even though you lost," he said, "I could tell the way you moved that you could fight. Could you stay in Miami for a couple weeks at my expense, so I could watch you train in the gym?"

With my ego crushed, my self-confidence at an all-time low, thinking, why should Angelo Dundee be interested in me, I declined his offer.

Could that have been Mr. Dundee on the other end of the phone that day or not? I'll never know, nor will it ever make a difference now. One can only imagine the possibilities.

After talking to whomever, Harry and I went out to see the sights of Miami nightlife. The next morning, we went to Howard Johnson's to have breakfast. Did I tell you Harry Arroyo is not only a great boxer, he's a comedian, too?

Sitting, eating breakfast on a Sunday morning in a restaurant that was packed full of people, he finished his breakfast first, stood up and grabbed his nose with his thumb and forefinger.

"Oh, Rusty, pee-you," he said, not very quietly. Then he started waving his hand around in the air as to fan away an odor, supposedly released by me. He then ran out of the restaurant, leaving me standing there, with the all the patrons looking at me, feeling totally embarrassed and stuck paying the bill. Nice guy, no? He did pay me back the full price of his breakfast later that day, though.

On another occasion, I got another good dose of humor. There was a fighter from the Pennsylvania Boxing Team, Alberto Collazzo, whom I met the previous year while training at Bulla Club in Sharon, Pa. He spoke very little English. I wanted to wish him luck on his fight taking place that evening.

Arroyo spoke Spanish fluently, so I asked him to tutor me on how to say, "Good luck on your fight tonight" in Spanish. After about five minutes of tutoring, I felt confident I could repeat what he taught me. Soon, I saw Alberto and signaled him to wait up. I wished him luck in Spanish—or so I thought!

Alberto got a real strange look on his face.

"What's wrong?" I asked.

"Why you tell me that?" he said to me.

"I just wanted to wish you luck in your fight tonight, in Spanish."

"No," he said, "you tell me to suck your ****."

I turned to confront Harry. I was mad enough to hit him for pulling such a prank. Sure enough, there he was, running down the hall, laughing.

"You can run now," I yelled to him, "but I'll catch up to you sooner or later, you dirty rat." All done in fun and no one, including Alberto, took offense at the joke.

I went back home, and back to the gym. I didn't want to face all the people who had believed in my ability and in me. I felt extremely bad and vowed to myself, no matter what, I would never have heart failure again.

CHAPTER 7

The Gold?

The 1976 National AAU Tournament was held in Las Vegas, Nevada, that year; and I wanted to go. Not only for the free trip but because I had something to prove to my fans, friends, the boxing world and, most importantly, to myself.

The Regional AAU Championships were held at the National Armory in Canton, Ohio, Rick Noggle's hometown. My good friend Terry Nicopolis traveled to the fights that night, along with my father, my brother, two buddies and my girlfriend. I got in line to be weighed in to find a big black guy in front of me. I can remember saying to myself, *My* God, *look at all the muscles on that guy.*

You could see every muscle in his body. He looked like a sculpture of clay, like a professional bodybuilder. While standing waiting for my turn to be weighed in, I remember saying to myself, *This man is so well-built he must be a light heavyweight. He's too tall and built too well to be only a middleweight. Thank* God! *I'd hate to have to fight him.*

Well, he stepped on the scales; and when I heard the official in charge of weighing in all the fighters say,

"Donaldson, 165," my heart stopped for a moment. Then it started beating fast, and my jaw dropped to my chest as I said silently to myself, *Oh, shit. I might have to fight this monster.*

Only four middleweights had entered the tournament: the muscleman; a no-name; Rick Noggle, the defending champ of two years and me. They put all four of our names in a hat and drew names out two at a time. Those two guys were to fight each other.

If you're thinking, *I bet he pulled muscleman for his first fight*, you are absolutely correct. I was fit to be tied! Just my luck! This guy's muscles started me thinking negatively again.

Terry saw the look on my face as the muscle man tipped the scales at exactly 165—the look of shock, that is. Not only was Terry a mountain of a man, he owned a heart that was bigger than his body size. He was a real motivator, supporter and a friend.

"Rusty," he told me at ringside, "you punch too hard for this guy. His legs aren't strong enough to withstand those right hands you throw."

Terry then instructed me to keep my left foot positioned between the other guy's feet.

"Wherever he goes, keep your distance and fight like you know how to fight. Throw lots of combinations, and box him smart."

After the introductions, we went back to our corners. Terry waited for me on the outside of the ring in my corner. As I walked back, I could hear him yelling, "Come on, champ! You're the best! Get out there and show the world what you can do!"

The bell rang for the start of the first round. I did as my trainers, Bob Miketa and Chuck Nelson, taught me; and, along with the advice I'd just gotten from my good friend Terry, I started measuring this hunk of a man up.

By the end of the first round, my opponent had felt my punching power on several occasions, and he started backpedaling. He was given two standing eight counts before the initial round finished.

The second round lasted only about one minute. I backed this guy up into a corner. I threw a three-punch combination, and all three punches landed solidly. The referee stepped in and gave him a standing eight count. As the fight resumed, I hit him with a perfect straight right hand, sending him through the ropes and out onto the tables put around ringside for the judges and officials. The referee helped him back into the ring, where he received another standing eight count.

The fight continued. I hit him with a left hook-right hand combination that put him down again. The referee, Pepper Martin, stopped the fight, awarding me the victory by raising my hand in the air. I had knocked out this mighty-looking man in the second round.

* * *

TKO Assures Noggle Rematch
Rosenberger Wins Bout

By Dave Kaminski

Local boxing fans have been wondering who is Rusty Rosenberger? About 1,200 of them had their question answered Thursday night as the Niles fighter stunned Dave Donaldson of Cleveland three times in the second round for a technical knockout in the semifinals of the Amateur Athletic Union (AAU) Lake Erie boxing championships in Memorial Auditorium.

***

That win put me in the finals of the 1976 AAU Regional Championships. I fought for the title and rights to fight in the National Tournament in Las Vegas. The defending champ was none other than Rick Noggle from Canton, Ohio.

As the fight drew near, my mind was set on destroying Noggle in his hometown, in front of all his fans. When I fought and beat him in Cleveland a month earlier, he had told the newspapers he thought he had won. After viewing the film taken of our fight, it clearly showed I out-pointed him, out-punched him and totally dominated the bout. I was going to make sure that no doubt would be in his or anyone else's mind about who won our second go-around.

I planned on knocking him out.

***

When we arrived at the Canton National Armory, one of the boxing officials handed me a newspaper printed that day. The headlines read, "Noggle to Defend Title after Mother's Funeral." Apparently, his mother had passed away recently after a long battle with cancer.

I felt terrible for Rick. How could I even think about fighting if my mother had died? I continued reading the article, and it went on to quote Rick. He stated, "My mother would have wanted me to fight tonight. She came to all my fights and cheered me on. I'm going to fight and beat Rusty, for my mother."

My whole outlook on fighting Rick that night changed. I am a fighter, and I can knock someone unconscious during a fight and still sleep very well at night. But I did have feelings, feelings of sympathy for Rick and this untimely death of his mother.

When the fight began, with the thoughts of Rick's mother's death fresh in my mind, I let the first round slip away, fighting in a very subdued way. When I sat down in the corner on my stool, Bob screamed at me, "What are you doing out there? You want to lose this fight, and lose your chance to show the world that getting beat by Sullivan in Miami was a fluke? That you are the best in the nation?"

I remember lowering my head. Bob smacked me right in the face, and said, "If you don't start fighting this round, I'm going to throw the towel in. You lose."

When he said those words "you lose,"—man, did that wake me up. I came out firing lefts and rights in combinations. I hit Rick so many times, so hard, I thought the referee should have stopped the fight, or at least given him a standing eight count. Nonetheless, I won a unanimous decision, and I was on my way to Las Vegas.

* * *

Rosenberger Wins in Split; Heads to Vegas

Canton—Rusty Rosenberger, the 165-pound boxing star with Warren RB Club, advanced to the National AAU Tournament in Las Vegas, Nev., May 10-15 after winning a split decision over Massillon's Rick Noggle here at Memorial Auditorium last night. The 20-year-old Nilesite was out to prove on Noggle's turf that his win over the Massillon fighter in Cleveland Golden Gloves last month was no fluke.

Rosenberger became the slugging

aggressor in the opening three minutes with his lefts to the head and rights to the body. Noggle, 23, scored on his share of punches, but Rosenberger's speed along with a final flurry at the bell earned him the round and the fight.

* * *

Look out, world, here I come!

On the plane ride to Las Vegas, I sat with the Light heavyweight Champ of Cleveland, Pablo (Paul) Ramos. We talked all the way to Vegas, mostly about Rick Noggle. He and Rick had become friends last year while they both fought in the nationals. Paul and I decided to room together while in Vegas.

When we landed in Las Vegas, I was impressed with all the bright lights, the casinos, the thousands of people. Pablo wore a big afro—in fact, "big" doesn't describe it. He picked his hair out so much he had trouble getting through doorways without his hair touching the sides or the top.

I remember riding in a taxicab, and the driver asking him to lock the door and lean on it so he could see out of his rearview mirror. At the time, it seemed humorous.

We enjoyed ourselves, gambled a little, walked for miles to see as many sights and casinos as possible. It left an impression on me as something really special, everything I had ever imagined and seen on TV. The weather was very hot but felt different from the heat back home, more of a dry, arid heat. I can remember taking a five-mile run and not even sweating upon completion. It truly amazed me.

The fights were held at the Las Vegas Convention Center, a huge building with three rings set up inside with fights going on in all three rings, all at the same time. On the first night of competition I was matched up against the number seven-ranked middleweight in the nation from the 1975 National AAU Tournament. I disposed of him in the first round using my favorite technique, the phantom right hand.

On the second night, I drew the number-one amateur middleweight in the world. He'd won the All-Service Championships, won the 1975 AAU Nationals, he fought against all the top countries in the world. He beat the Polish, Cuban and Russian national boxing champs. The USA Olympic Committee had groomed him for the last four years in preparation for the 1976 Olympic Games. He fought and beat Michael Spinks, the 1976 Olympic Gold Medalist, in the Pan-American Games in 1975, winning a unanimous decision over three rounds. This outstanding boxer and Olympic hopeful's name: Thomas Brooks.

I think it could have been a conspiracy. In the Golden Gloves Nationals in Miami I was matched up against the defending champ. Now, I was going up against the best amateur middleweight in the world.

Remembering the "heart attack" I'd suffered fighting Sullivan, I put my head down and started to mentally prepare myself to fight the best amateur fighter in the world.

I was gloved up, ready to go on and fight. I was standing in the vicinity of the corner of the ring that I was to be fighting out of. I was looking at the ring, and the referee was raising the hand of the winner of the previous fight. Someone—it could even have been you, or maybe just a sign from God—but someone walked up behind me and tapped me on the right shoulder.

Without turning around, I said, "Yeah, what's up?"

"Be careful," this person told me. "He has a good right hand."

I nodded my head forward, and said, "Thanks."

I climbed into the ring, and for the first time saw the best amateur middleweight in the world. According to the ratings, he had fought and beaten all the other best amateur fighters in the world.

When the referee gave the pre-fight instructions, Brooks didn't even look at me. He just kept moving his head side-to-side, giving me the impression that I didn't concern him. The bell rang, starting the fight. I danced towards him. He threw a sharp left jab. I saw it coming, slipped it and countered with my own jab to his midsection.

I stepped back to make distance between us. He stepped to me and threw a second jab. I again slipped it and countered with another jab to his midsection.

As I slipped his second jab, I noticed that he flinched his right hand, as if he wanted to throw it, but he didn't. I danced backwards. He stepped towards me, throwing a third jab.

In a flash, I thought, "That person told me just before the fight he has a good right hand. He'll probably try to use it now."

I was right. He threw a third jab; and here it came, that right hand, like a missile heading directly towards my jaw. I slid underneath it, hitting him with my own stiff right hand to the body, driving him back into the ropes. As he was lying on the ropes, I stepped in and hit him with four straight punches to his chest and facial area. When I had delivered those four punches, with him leaning into the ropes and the ropes having tension, I took a step back, making space between us.

He stepped forward with speed and force, coming off the ropes. I moved towards him. He held his left hand high, protecting the left side of his face. I again moved forward, bending my knees slightly, looking at his stomach, making him think I was going to throw another body shot.

With us inches a part, he lowered his left hand to block the body punch he thought I was about to throw, leaving his chin wide open. In a split-second decision, I threw a fast, hard, picture-perfect straight right hand that landed squarely on his unprotected chin.

That was all he could handle. You could have counted to a hundred. He wasn't moving—and didn't move until someone administered smelling salts to bring him back to existence. I had just knocked out the best middleweight in the world, in the *first round*!

Michael Spinks owes me a debt of gratitude. In the amateurs, the rules state if you are knocked out during a fight it's mandatory to take one month off from any contact. Two weeks following the AAU Nationals in Las Vegas, the Olympic trials began in Cincinnati, Ohio. When Thomas Brooks fought me and I knocked him out in the first round, it eliminated him from participating in the Olympic tryouts, putting him out of contention for the 1976 Olympic gold.

My third fight in as many nights matched me up against a hard-punching kid from Chicago, Illinois, named Leroy Murphy. I was standing in my corner moments before the opening bell. My two trainers, Bob Miketa and Chuck Nelson, were arguing over the way I should go out and fight this guy. Bob wanted me to fight the same style I had used the previous two fights. Chuck wanted me to go out and slug with the guy.

While they were arguing in the corner, the bell sounded, but with the noise from the crowd and my trainers screaming at each other I didn't hear it. The referee walked over and said, "Box." I turned around to look for my opponent, but he had already found me standing in my corner. As I was turning, Leroy hit me with a blindside right hand, knocking me down to one knee.

That was the first time I had been knocked off my feet while fighting in the ring. Instead of thinking, I reacted by jumping up as fast as I could. The referee gave me a standing eight count. The war commenced.

We fought each other like life or death. We both landed many hard, punishing blows.

In 1976, headgear became optional. Leroy wore one until the third round. A right-hand bomb exploded on the side of his head and tore his headgear off. The punch sent the headgear flying out of the ring to hit a spectator walking by ringside.

The bell rang, ending the fight. Leroy just lay on the ropes with a faraway look in his eyes. I walked over to him and escorted him back to his corner, then returned to mine. I was in the blue corner, and Leroy was in the red. The referee motioned for us to come to the center of the ring for the announcing of the winner.

I made it to the center, giving my hand to the referee. I looked over and saw that Leroy was still in his corner, still dazed, unaware of his actions. I walked over to his corner and led him out to the referee.

The announcer said, "The winner, in the blue corner," and the referee began to raise my hand, until the announcer said, "Leroy Murphy." There seemed to be a lot of confusion and booing when they awarded him the victory.

I made it back to the locker room and one of the officials, Rolly Swartz, came to me and said, "You, in fact, won the fight on the three judges' score cards. Since the decision had already been given to the public, it will go in the books as such, a victory for Murphy."

He advised me to "Go home and have a passport made. The Olympic Committee wants to send you to London, England, to fight on the USA Boxing Team."

Returning home somewhat of a winner for my demolition of the best amateur middleweight in the world, I went and got a passport made as advised.

Bob and his wife stayed in Las Vegas on a second honeymoon for two weeks following the AAU National

Tournament. They hadn't gone on a honeymoon when they first married. During this two-week span of time, the Olympic Committee changed their minds again. They decided that, since I had knocked out the number-one amateur middleweight in the world in one round, and had been royally cheated out of a decision I had justly won and a possible national title, they would invite me to participate in the Olympic tryouts.

They sent the application form to Bob Miketa's home address instead of mine. The day Bob returned home from Las Vegas happened to be the first day of the trials.

I remember well sitting in front of the TV watching Leo Randolph fighting in the Olympic trials, the whole time wishing I could be there fighting. The phone rang. It was Bob. He informed me he had just pulled in from the airport and took all the mail out of his mailbox.

"You'll never believe what I found in my mailbox," he said.

"Letters and bills, right?" I said.

"There is an application form for the Olympic tryouts, you're supposed to be there." Timing in life is everything. Bad timing cost me a chance to be recorded in history.

I didn't let that stop me, though. I was through having heart failures. I had taken my first step, and it would soon be time for me to take another, bigger step.

CHAPTER 8

Enter Lou Duva

I was in the gym training. Moe Harvey was there, too, watching me and the other fighters also working out. I was a little depressed because of the recent events in my boxing career.

After I finished, I sat down at the table; and Moe sat down with me. He lit up a cigarette, and I asked him if he knew any professional boxing managers.

Moe told me he knew Ernie Shavers' manager Black Genero, who was from Youngstown, Ohio. He also had dealings with a light heavyweight named John Jorowski. John had fought a hard-punching fighter from New Jersey by the name of Christy Elliot. A guy named Lou Duva managed Mr. Elliot, and Moe had been in contact with Lou. He wrote Duva's name and phone number on a piece of paper and gave it to me.

I was excited. Moe didn't give those numbers to just anybody. The fact that he gave it to me meant he though I had a good shot at making it as a pro. I was too excited, in fact.

That night, driving my two-year-old Corvette home, I came to a red light. I glanced down at the passenger's seat where I had laid Moe's piece of paper. I was so excited, concentrating on Lou Duva's name and phone number on this piece of paper, that I forgot to watch out for the car in front of me. I ran right into the back of this guy's car! Fortunately for me, I wasn't going fast enough to do any damage to his vehicle or mine.

I made contact with Lou Duva over the phone. I wanted to become the middleweight champ of the world; and if Duva was to be believed, he had the connections to get me there. We agreed for me to drive up to New Jersey and work out in his gym so he could get a first-hand look at my boxing skills.

I drove to New Jersey via Interstate 80 through Pennsylvania to New Jersey. I arrived safely, and he had reserved a hotel room for me at the Holiday Inn. I got settled in and called my mother to let her know I made it; I called Lou to tell him I had arrived.

He said, "Give me an hour, I'll come pick you up, and I'll take you to dinner and talk."

The hour flew by. It seemed like it was only five minutes until I heard someone knocking on the door. The first thing I saw when I answered was a heavyset man. He wore a big smile that showed off his perfectly aligned white teeth. He might not have taken care of his body the way he should, but he sure took care of his teeth.

Lou took me out to dinner in New York City. What a thrill! It was the first time in my life I had ever been in NYC. He took me a real classy restaurant by the name of Gallagher's. According to Lou, it was one of the best steak houses in the world.

While sitting waiting to have my T-bone steak served to me, I look around the restaurant and as I scanned the dining room, I finished taking my survey of the place by looking over at a guy sitting right next to me. When I looked at his plate to see what he was eating my eyes almost popped out of the sockets.

This man was eating a steak rare. It was so rare that his steak was actually lying in a plateful of blood. As I watched him cut a piece, when he put downward pressure on his knife while cutting blood flowed out it like it was a fresh kill. I told you it was rare.

Not only did he eat every bite of that steak, he tore off pieces of bread, soaked up the remaining blood on his plate and ate that also.

At dinner, Lou told me of all the fighters he had managed in the past, like Christy Elliott and a heavyweight named Scott Franks. He continued by saying, "Scott is the next white hope. Those niggers are taking over everything, and I'm tired of it."

He told me if I wanted to be successful in this business I'd have to learn how to play ball with the big boys. I wasn't exactly sure what he meant by that statement, at the time.

The next day he picked me up and took me to a gym located in downtown Patterson, New Jersey. It was directly over top of a tailor's shop that his brother owned and operated. It was a small gym, and the ring was even smaller—the smallest ring I've ever seen, in fact. When I asked the size of the ring, Lou said, "It's about ten by ten"—a "puncher's ring," he called it.

Two black guys showed up to test my skills. They appeared to be really rugged characters: unshaven, greasy hair, and with an odor about them I could smell from across the room. One was an accomplished fighter. He showed good skills and seemed to be in decent shape. The other guy I busted up big time.

I guess Lou liked what he saw because he told me of the connections he had with the USA Boxing Team. He told me he was going to get me some international fights.

He held true to his word. I returned to Ohio and received

a phone call from him a short time later. He informed me he had me set to fight in Bermuda. Man, I was excited! I was going to Bermuda to fight? This guy must really have some connections!

Of course, I accepted. I packed up, got on the plane and off I went! Bob even went with me.

When I landed in Bermuda and stepped off the plane, it felt so humid I could hardly breathe. Almost everyone was black, though that didn't bother me. I was given a hero's welcome and a beautiful hotel room overlooking the ocean.

Then, it was fight time, and I found out that the guy I was scheduled to fight was a white hairdresser who stood six feet, five inches tall. His name was Gary Cope. Being that tall and only weighing one hundred sixty-five pounds, you can imagine how thin he was.

I entered the ring. The bell rang to start the fight. I found out quickly that he could jab fast but had no power. I have to admit, in the first round he landed more jabs to my face than anyone else had ever been able to do.

In the second round, I had got my punching range down and landed some atom bombs. To my surprise, he withstood my hardest punches and never left his feet. Without any doubt in my mind or Bob's, I had dominated this tall, thin man the last two rounds of the fight.

Then the announcer read the decision. They had me losing! I'm telling you, the crowd went crazy! They booed nonstop for at least fifteen minutes, throwing their programs into the ring to protest the bad decision.

I talked to Duva later that night on the phone. He replied, "Don't worry about it, next time they want me to send them down a fighter I'll send them a mean-ass nigger to knock their hairdresser out."

Fellow Duva managee John Mitchell had accompanied me. He lived in Windham, Ohio, a little town way out in the country. He must have been fed really well, because he was big and strong and really packed a stick of dynamite in his right hand. He fought an Olympic medalist named Virgil Hill, born and bred in Bermuda, and lost on a second-round TKO.

Next thing I knew, Lou was calling me again to fight on the USA Boxing Team. This time, I was going to fight someone from the Russian National Boxing Team in Milwaukee, Wisconsin.

Bob and I flew to Milwaukee and got settled in. The Russian coaches somehow had heard of my boxing accomplishments. They told the USA officials that they'd rather I fight their junior middleweight instead. The USA officials agreed to the fight, which had also been agreed on by Lou first.

As it turned out, this junior middleweight fighter from Russia had fought in the past two Olympic Games, winning a gold medal on both occasions. As Bob and I were leaving the hotel room, the phone rang. It was Lou. He told me, "This guy you're going to fight is pretty good, tough and experienced. If he knocks you down, get up and do the best you can to protect yourself."

Thanks a lot, Lou. My confidence level took a nosedive. I was about to fight a two-time Olympic Gold Medalist, and my manager offered no words of encouragement.

To get to the ring, I had to walk down a flight of cement block steps, through the Russian dressing room and out to the arena. As Bob and I walked down these huge, wide, concrete steps, they were actually shaking. At the same time, we heard a pounding noise. As we neared the bottom of the steps, there stood my Russian opponent. He was warming up by hitting the wall adjacent to the staircase, shaking the concrete steps.

As we walked by him, he stopped punching the wall, looked at me and said in broken English, "I gonna knock you out."

My first reaction was *Oh, shit*. Then I thought back to when I had chickened out fighting Sullivan in Florida. I continued walking to the ring. If I told you that I wasn't scared, I'd be lying to you. I was real scared. With what Lou had told me on the phone, this guy had proven he was the best in the world for the past eight years. *Yes*, I was scared, but I was also sure that I was going to fight this Russian the best I possibly could.

The referee gave the pre-fight instructions, mine in English and his in Russian. The ring announcer had earlier made the announcement that this referee also was from Russia. The bell rang, and we met in the center of the ring.

My jab worked well. Early on, he fired a big left hook at my head, but I saw it coming and slipped it nicely. I threw a right hand to the body then back on top with a left hook, both punches landing with a crash. He shrugged it off by moving his head back and forth as to say "No, the punches didn't bother me."

I threw another left jab; but he anticipated and slipped it. He unleashed a powerful left uppercut of his own towards my stomach, only it landed south of the border. I immediately felt pain, dropping to one knee.

The Russian referee came to me, grabbed me by my elbows and lifted me upright. He then shook his head no and said, "Box." I was still bent half over!

My Russian opponent reached in and hit me with a sledgehammer right hand right behind my left earlobe. It appeared to me as though I rode on a fast turning merry-go-round. The whole place spun around and around until I lost my balance and my ass hit the canvas.

The referee started counting: one, two, three, I got up at the count of eight totally on reflex—I had no idea where I was or what I was doing. The referee wisely stopped the fight. Well, that Russian fighter had kept his word—he told me he was going to knock me out, and he did.

Lou Duva created a boxing team for New Jersey that had the best fighters in the state representing it. He named the boxing team the Jersey Gladiators. To mention a few of the Gladiators, they included Scott Franks, heavyweight; Rusty Rosenberger, middleweight; Nino Gonzales, welterweight, and Gerald Hayes, lightweight.

Exactly one week later to the day, I was in New Jersey; Lou had me scheduled for another fight. The Jersey Gladiators, representing the USA Boxing Team, were going to fight the national boxing team from Ireland.

I asked Lou how I could fight, since I had been stopped by the Russian only a week earlier. Wasn't it mandatory I take off one month according to the AAU rules?

He answered, "Don't worry about it, I'll take care of everything."

My opponent would be the middleweight with the most international competition experience—in other words, he had scored more wins fighting fighters from other countries than any other fighter on the Irish National Boxing Team.

My brother, Razor, Nick Francos and I drove up to New Jersey for the fight show. Nick was a friend of mine, a twelve-year-old kid who liked boxing and trained at the same gym as I did. He may have been only twelve years old, but he was strong and he could punch. After my workouts in the gym, I'd stand in one of the corners, and, after gloving him up, let Nick pound away on my stomach. It helped strengthen my abs and let Nick practice throwing punches.

It also helped to build a close friendship with the kid. Nick was a first-class boy with two very loving parents. His parents owned a bar in Warren, Ohio, called the Buena Vista Cafe. They served liquor and food. His dad's name was also Nick, and Nick Sr. specialized in a chicken dinner called "Uncle Nick's Greek Fried Chicken." His logo: "If the Colonel had my recipe, he'd be a General."

I can't tell you how many times, after a workout at the gym, Razor and I would give Nick Jr. a ride to the Buena Vista and then go in and have dinner, on the house. It was a special time in my boxing history that I'll carry in my heart to the grave. Mr. and Mrs. Francos and Nick are some of the finest people on God's great earth. Thanks for the wonderful memories.

Before the show began, I was walking around the arena like I usually did before a fight. It helped me loosen my muscles and relax my nerves. My sister Terri and her husband George Anthony traveled to New Jersey from their home in Niles, Ohio, and were seated ringside. I spotted them from across the room, or should I say across the school gymnasium. The name of the school: Kennedy High School, located in Patterson, New Jersey. The date of this event: February 19, 1977.

I walked over to greet them, and George had a worried look on his face. I asked him what was bothering him.

He told me, "While sitting here, I talked to a couple guys from Ireland. They told me about this tough guy you're about to fight. He's scored a couple KOs during his international competition, and he's the Ireland National Champ. No one in his country can beat him. Rusty, I hope you're ready. It sounds like you're in for a tough fight."

"I made it through alive fighting the Russian last week," I said reassuringly. "I'll be all right, you'll see."

The pre-fight show impressed all the fight fans. The Irish National Boxing Team emerged from their locker room and marched out all in a row. One by one they entered the ring and lined up, starting with the heavyweight first, who carried a flagpole displaying the Irish National Flag, and continuing right on down to the flyweight.

Then the USA team entered the ring, with all the fighters color-coordinated in their red-white-and-blue uniforms. Scott Franks, our heavyweight, carried Old Faithful into the ring for the Jersey Gladiators, representing the USA National Boxing Team. I've never felt that proud as I did standing there ready to represent my country.

The announcer introduced each fighter, first the Irish fighter, then the USA fighter of the same weight. When the two were introduced, the fighters met in the center of the ring, shook hands and exchanged a small gift. My opponent gave me an Irish pin that displayed the Ireland National flag, a stickpin-type ornament you fasten on the jacket of your boxing uniform that indicates all the different countries you've fought against.

I, in turn, gave him the same kind of stickpin, only, of course, it displayed the American flag and colors, The *red, white and blue*—have I mentioned that I'm proud to be an American?

The opening ceremonies lasted about half an hour, but it seemed like only minutes. Then, it was time to rumble. After being crushed by my Russian opponent exactly one week before, I felt relaxed, confident and strong going into this fight. All the pressure was off. The only way for me to go was up.

The bell rang to begin the contest. I danced out of my corner to meet my opponent. His footwork was the first thing I noticed. He fought with his right foot directly behind his left—I mean *directly* behind his left. If he fought on a balance beam, he would have been able to balance himself perfectly.

Only he wasn't on a balance beam, but in a boxing ring, where you can open up you stance by spreading your feet. Doing this, it will give you speed of foot, perfect balance, additional punching power and better overall body control. After a quick survey of his foot positioning, I immediately started moving in a circle. Obviously, for this guy to get off any punches, his opponent would need to be directly in front of him. I decided to use the angle approach.

My footwork, hand speed and punching power proved to be too much for my Irish friend. I picked him apart. I hit him with every conceivable punch in the book. To his credit, he withstood a barrage of hard, accurate punches to the body, face and chin.

He did land his share of punches to my facial area. The top of his head found my eyebrows a number of times throughout the fight. The Irish referee in control of our match warned him on several occasions to keep his head up. Fortunately for me, my skin remained in one piece, no cuts.

Other than a standing eight count given to him in the third round, he never showed any signs of giving up. I'll say this much for my friend from Ireland, he proved to be a gutsy guy.

After the last fight of the show, the official gave a special award to the most outstanding fighter on either team. There were a total of twelve fighters on the USA team, and twelve fighters on the Irish team. The award was named the James J. Braddock Award, and only one trophy was to be awarded to the fighter who had shown himself to be exceptional.

I won the award, a beautiful three-foot-tall trophy for being the best fighter on either team. My ego may have been bruised fighting the Russians the week before, but that week I shone. Thank you, *Lord*!

CHAPTER 9

Paid for Punch

The date of my first professional fight was January 19, 1978; and it was to be held in Bergen, New Jersey. I was excited. I was going to be paid for doing what I loved to do the most—box. I felt so excited that I couldn't sleep the night before the fight.

The bout was scheduled to be a four-round contest, but it didn't last that long. When I hit my opponent with the phantom punch, out went the lights. Before the curtain came crashing down on this guy, he did manage to land one or two jabs to my face, but left no telling marks—no cuts, no black eyes. The unfortunate fellow's name was Ray Garcia, my first victim of many, I hoped.

The next fight was scheduled for February 23, 1978, in the same place as my pro debut. Could lightning strike twice in the same spot?

When Gene Muldrow, my opponent, entered the ring, he appeared to be somewhat out of shape. His body wasn't tight—he had no real muscle definition—but he had some ring experience and held on for four rounds of punishment. Muldrow was one of those fighters who lead with his head—the top of his head, to be exact. He head-butted me several times. I must have tough skin, though, for it left no marks or cuts to my face. I earned a four-round decision.

My third professional fight was to be held in my old stomping grounds, the Struthers Field House in Youngstown, Ohio, on April 26, 1978. I was billed as the co-feature on this fight card. My friend from Cleveland, Pablo Ramos, was billed as the main event; and it was a good thing. He went through eight good, solid rounds, with plenty of exciting boxing action. He won on a unanimous decision.

My fight lasted less than thirty seconds. I hit Earnie Wicher with a hook-right hand combination, putting him down and out on the canvas. I initially thought the guy quit on me, until I walked over to his corner to shake hands and make sure he was okay. When I got to his corner, he sat on his chair, holding an ice bag on his left temple.

I asked him, "Are you all right?"

He removed the ice bag to reposition it, revealing a huge knot right on his left temple area.

On May 20, 1978, I fought a guy who, from Lou's description, was going to be a tough fight—real tough. He'd won a few amateur championships and was supposed to be a real banger, a hard puncher and a good boxer.

When I tell you I trained hard for this fight, I don't want you to think that I didn't train hard for all my fights, amateur and professional, because I did. When I say I trained hard, I not only mean physically but mentally. I woke up in the morning thinking about it. I did my roadwork thinking about it. I showered thinking about it. Driving in my car I'd be thinking about it. I even made love thinking about it.

At night I lay in my bed thinking about it, I'd throw punches in the air and envision myself in the ring fighting this man. Some nights, I'd jump out of bed and start shadow boxing, break a sweat and have to shower all over again before I could get back in bed to try and sleep.

After a fifteen- or twenty-minute shadow boxing workout, my adrenaline was pumping pretty hard. I wanted to be the champ of the world real bad, and this was the only way I could get there. I was so focused on this fight that I would often just stare into space until my work partner and good friend Jeff would say, "Rusty, Rusty, snap out of it man, your scaring me."

He'd at times grab me by my shoulders and shake me to snap me out of my self-induced coma.

In this state of self-hypnosis, I'd continually say to myself, "You can't lose. You're the best. You can't lose. You won't. You're the champ."

I'd be willing to bet my last dollar that there hasn't been anyone in the history of boxing who wanted it more than I. I had the talent, elite conditioning, dedication, desire, attitude, intelligence and time. I was only twenty-three years old.

The fight was scheduled against Billy Perez in Trenton, New Jersey. I arrived at the site of the fight show and did my usual. I found the locker room, dropped off my gym bag and boxing apparel and weighed in. I was scheduled to fight fourth on the card.

Bob wanted to wrap my hands early on this night because he wanted to go out and watch the show. My friend Jeff and I walked around the arena, talking to each other about this tough guy I was about to fight.

"How can you fight?" Jeff asked me. "Man, I'm nervous, and I'm not even fighting."

"I've been fighting so long and have had so many fights that it's no big deal," I told him. "I train hard, I know how to fight. Tonight's fight does have me a little nervous, though. Lou knows fighters, and he's never lied to me yet. If he says this guy's tough—well, I'm counting on a hard fight tonight."

As we were walking around this place, we came up on two girls standing by a pay phone. One of the girls was talking on the phone. Just then, Bob joined us.

"The second fight is just starting," he said. "As soon as it's over you better come get warmed up."

Jeff and I stopped when Bob approached us. When he finished talking, we were standing close to these two girls near the phone. Before we walked away, the girl that wasn't on the phone looked at my wrapped hands and asked, "Who are you fighting tonight?"

"Billy Perez," I told her.

She lets out a loud, high-pitched yell and said something in Spanish.

"No comprende," I said.

"You are in big trouble tonight, man," she said in broken English. "You are fighting my boy, and he going to knock you out, put you to sleep. You better think about fighting my boy, he going to get you."

I looked at her, smiled, turned and walked away.

As we were walking, Jeff asked me, "Man, didn't that scare you?"

"Perez may have knocked out some of his opponents," I told him, "but he's not going to knock me out. I guarantee you one thing, Jeff. He's going to know he was in a fight. You'll see."

At fight time, someone left open the butterfly cage that was in my stomach again. We got the pre-fight instructions from the referee, touched gloves and headed back to our respective corners. I reached mine first and turned to watch Perez move.

As he was walking back to his corner, unaware that I was watching, he was shadow boxing, warming up. I immediately noticed that every time he threw a left jab his right hand dropped down around his neck. That was stored in my memory.

The bell rang, and I danced out to meet this man in combat. He threw the first jab at me. I took a step backward, making space between us; and, at the same time, I looked at his right hand. Sure enough, he dropped it—just a little bit, but it did come down. I remember saying to myself, *As the fight goes on and he starts getting winded, I bet that right hand will drop even lower.*

In the first round, I concentrated on establishing my jab and landing hard, solid right hands to his body and face. The combination that was landing and working well for me was the right hand to the body, left hook to the head. I'd throw in a foot-feint or two every now and again, keeping him off-balance and making him guess what I was about to throw next.

When Lou had told me he was tough, I think he meant that this guy was able to endure a lot of punishment. In the second round, he threw a jab at me. I took a small step back with my left foot and dipped my head slightly to my left. His jab passed my face. He had committed his jab to full extension. I countered with a crushing left hook over his lowered right hand directly into his chin. The look in his eyes was as if he'd seen a ghost, but it was too late. He had an appointment with the canvas, and my left hook was his ride there.

Down but not out, he still had some fight left in him. After he rose, my punches landed with power, and often. In the third round, the phantom punch found its mark and left its calling card. He threw a left jab at me. I reacted by dropping my right foot backwards just enough to make his jab miss me then immediately countered over top of his missed jab with a hard, powerful right hand. He went down like someone had opened a trap door in the ring floor.

As he lay on the canvas, he put both of his gloved hands up to his head and started crying like a little baby and saying, "Oh, my head, oh, my head hurts."

He was carried out of the ring and back to the dressing room, where his head was packed in ice for a period of time. It took him a while, but he recovered.

***

Rosenberger stops 4th foe

Trenton, N.J—Warren middleweight boxer Rusty Rosenberger picked up his fourth win in as many fights with a TKO victory over Billy Perez at Notre Dame High School here Tuesday.

Perez failed to answer the bell for the third round, giving the 165-pound Rosenberger his third KO decision in his short professional career.

***

My fifth fight, on June 13, 1978, was the first real test of my pro career. The site of my fourth fight was the Ice World in Totowa, New Jersey. I was scheduled to fight a guy who had just gotten out of the army. While in the service, he'd won the All-Army Championship. He was a little taller than I, but built thinner.

Dan Stahle was fighting his pro debut, and I could tell by looking at his physique he had trained hard. He looked as tight as a drum. Nothing jiggled on his body. I knew he would give me a good fight.

He was a good boxer, moved well on his feet, and had fast hands. His punching power wasn't that hard, though he did land more jabs than I would have liked. In the third round, the phantom punch landed with power. To my surprise, it didn't knock him down initially. I immediately came right back and hit him with a right hand-left hook combination that put him down for an eight count. He got up and absorbed a couple more hard punches and a right uppercut just as the bell ended the third round.

He walked back to his corner a little wobbly but made it to his chair for a much-needed minute break from the action. The next three rounds he danced, ran, jabbed and ran some more. Every time we got close, he'd tie me up and hold on for dear life. I took my share of jabs and right hands—quick, snappy punches but with not much sting on them. Although I did get head-butted on two occasions and absorbed more jabs than I cared to, my skin remained intact—no cuts or bruises.

At Ice World, whenever Lou held a show, he would have programs made to sell to the attending fight fans. In the programs, he had the history of the boxers fighting that evening. You know—their win/loss records and a short summary of each fighter particulars. The following is what was reported about me and my boxing career up to that point:

> Rosenberger actually has grabbed more notice in his local appearances then more publicized stablemate Scott Frank! And for good reason, too—fast hands, continual pressure, and lots of heart. Rusty had no easy opponent June 13th when he had to take a 6-round nod over Dan Staehle, showing all those attributes.
>
> Compact, Rosenberger impressed with his no-nonsense professional effort, few of the wild blows you'd expect from a new paid boxer, excellent pacing though never sitting on the lead. He was busy all the time

> and took some good punches on the chin from Staehle. In tonight's fight, Rosenberger is favored to win, within the distance, using his sharp combinations to jolt White into a TKO around the 3rd or 4th. Rusty just has too many guns for his opponent tonight.

Lou scheduled me to fight again on July 18, 1978, in Totowa, NJ. I was to fight against Harry White. He didn't last long at all. The very first jab he threw at me, I bent my knees slightly and tilted my head to the right to let his jab go by my face and along the left side. With perfect timing of my legs, head, shoulders and fist, I countered with the prettiest right hand you've ever saw. He went down and out in a hurry.

On this day not only did I fight but there was also a big newspaper story done on me and my career.

* * *

On August 17, 1978, I fought again in Totowa, New Jersey. I was scheduled to fight an amateur champ whose name was Greg Duran. I knocked him out in the second round of the scheduled six-rounder.

Next, I was to fight at Beaver County Community College, near Pittsburgh, Pa. On August 22, 1978, the fight was held in an arena that was named the Gold Dome. It was a big, beautiful gold dome built right on the college campus for seminars, basketball games and concerts. It was a very impressive piece of architecture.

My opponent originally was supposed to be Sam Long, but he developed a bad case of chicken wings and pulled out the night before the scheduled six-round bout. The promoter did some fast shuffling, and they came up with an opponent for me by the name of Ron Beverage. Sam Long must have known something that Ron Beverage didn't. Only thirty seconds into the first round, the phantom right hand did the job once again, knocking Beverage out in the first round: a cold Beverage.

I drove back to my home away from home the very next day. I fought again on August 30, 1978, in Paramus, New Jersey, at the Imperial Manor. My opponent was Bam Bam Ramsey; this fight was stopped two minutes and fifteen seconds into the third round.

My professional record stood at nine wins and no losses, with seven knockouts. My popularity was increasing with the fight fans of New Jersey, though I was not too popular with my past opponents.

Lou had an uncanny way of picking fights for all his fighters, including me. Of my first nine opponents, seven of them were fights I was supposed to score knockouts in, or at least win relatively easily. They weren't the same caliber of fighter as I. That's how a smart manager picks and chooses fights for his prospect. It builds the prospect's record and gives him experience, fine-tuning his skills in the ring.

Every once in a while, though, the manager takes a calculated risk and ups the quality of fighter he has his prospect fight. Lou had an expertly trained eye for good prospects, like a sixth sense.

The next fight was on October 19, 1978; it was going to be held in Garfield, New Jersey. I was scheduled to fight a man from Philadelphia by the name of Bobby Day. My arsenal was complete. By then, there wasn't a punch I couldn't throw with accuracy, speed and power. Mr. Day was stopped in the third round with a crushing body shot to the liver. It was my tenth victory in as many outings, and I'd had no need for a cut man yet. Thank you, Lord.

My next fight was to be held at the Felt Forum, right beside Madison Square Garden. The fight program read,

"Rusty Rosenberger seems to have a problem. Whenever the middleweight from Niles, Ohio, has a bout, his opponent contracts Parkinson's disease of the chin."

My hometown newspaper ran a feature story on me and my boxing career I'd like to share with you.

* * *

Rusty Still on Track

By Larry Ringler
Tribune Sports Writer,
September 3, 1978

> *Rusty Rosenberger has come a long way since the day he walked into the Niles, Ohio, YMCA gym and decided he wanted to become a boxer.*
>
> *Now he's an undefeated professional with 11 wins under the elastic waistband of his trunks. He trains in a New Jersey camp and frequently works out in the fabled Gleason's Gymnasium in New York City.*
>
> *And, at 22 years of age, the Niles, Ohio, native is on the verge of fighting in the Camelot of boxing—Madison Square Garden.*
>
> *Rosenberger is one of the many young middleweights trying to scale the ranks. The goal is always the same—the championship. And the methods seldom vary: fight anyone you can as often as you can.*
>
> *The road to establishing your name and ability is long and tough. But those closest*

to Rosenberger say he's got what it takes to do it.

"I feel he has the tools and the potential to be a top contender," says his trainer of six years, Bob Miketa. "All he needs to do is build his record a bit and he'll get the right shot."

"I would say Rusty is one of the top middleweights in the United States,' declares his father Ray. "If anybody can win the championship, he has the ability and class to do it. When he sets out to do something, he doesn't deviate from his course. I'm sure that if he gets a chance to fight in the Garden, he'll be popular with the fans.

Rosenberger hasn't been popular with his opponents, however. Seven have gone down for the count. In his last two outings, his scheduled foes have failed to show for one reason or another, forcing the promoter to find a quick replacement.

So far his most impressive victory has been a six-round decision over former All-Army Champion Dan Staehle last June.

Rusty's career goes back to a rope tied between two giant oak trees in his backyard. His father, a former boxer in the Navy and a self-confessed "physical fitness nut," rigged the apparatus in order to help his boys develop their upper body strength.

The technique worked so well that when the gym teacher of Rusty's brother, Ray or Razor, asked him to do pushups one day, Razor didn't stop until he'd done 350.

Their father remembers the day his sons came to ask permission to begin their ring careers.

"I told them if they wanted to try it for a bit of self-protection, it would be all right with me," he said. "I thought that would be the extent of it. But they liked it and went on."

Bringing their mother, Helen, to their side was another problem entirely.

"My wife had reservations about it then and still does," Ray admitted.

"She was opposed to it at first. She didn't want them to get hurt or hurt anyone else. Even now she won't go to any of their fights. But we take movies all the time and she'll watch them. Even though she knows the outcome, she still cheers for them as if she's right there at ringside. I think she's accepted it now."

Both Rosenbergers took their first steps in boxing in the Golden Gloves amateur tournament in Youngstown, Ohio. Rusty won his class four straight years and in 1976 captured the regional AAU and GG championships in Cleveland. From there it was on to Las Vegas where he fought the number one ranked middleweight in the world, knocking him out in the opening round of the scheduled three round fight. He fought on the same canvas as current World Boxing Association Heavyweight Champion Leon Spinks and Olympic Gold Medalist Sugar Ray Leonard. Rusty got eliminated in a very unpopular decision going to Leroy

Murphy of Chicago, Ill. and wound up being rated sixth in the nation.

In the meantime, Rusty is training at his New Jersey camp awaiting word from his manager Lou Duva along with the officials from Madison square Garden on a possible fight. He runs five miles every morning, and then works out at least two hours in the gym.

Miketa, who first entered Rusty's career when the fighter was part of the Warren AC stable, is kept busy as well. He frequently flies from his Youngstown home to New Jersey to help Rusty in his training. To find the time, he uses most of his vacation time from Packard Electric.

Is it worth putting the human body through all this when you know the great odds against finally earning the right to be called "Champ?"

Right now, at the age of 22, there's no doubt in Rusty's mind.

* * *

I'll never forget that fight. It was held on December 15, 1978. I was fighting a Puerto-Rican boxer by the name of Angel Perales, who carried the reputation of being a good fighter. He was tall and had long arms that seemed to be able to reach clear across the ring.

During the weigh-ins, his father and brother talked trash, saying how tough and what great shape Angel conditioned himself into, with knock-out power in either hand. He and I even exchanged a few words.

"Rosenberger," he said, "I'm going to have you shipped back to Ohio in a body bag."

"You've done the easy part," I responded.

"What's that?" he asked.

"Talking," I said. I smiled at him and walked away.

During the pre-fight instructions the referee gave in the center of the ring, we stared intensely at each other. I attempted to touch gloves after the instructions by extending my hand out in sportsmanlike fashion. Without touching my glove, he looked me in the eyes and said, "Let's fight."

Though they called him "Angel," unfortunately for him, the Lord only bought him a second-class ticket. My jabs landed almost at will, my right hand didn't take long to find its mark and my hook was really working for me that night. I fought with grace and speed of foot and put on a punch slipping show that "Willie Pep" would have been proud of.

I think one reason I fought so well that night was that a former middleweight champ of the world, Emile Griffith, gave me a great rubdown just before this fight. He made my muscles so loose—I had never felt so relaxed before a fight.

The viewing audience showed their appreciation for my performance by giving me a nice round of applause. The referee raised my hand in victory, and the announcer spoke my name as the winner of the six-round contest by a unanimous decision.

My record at that point stood at eleven wins, no losses with nine knockouts. I held the ranking of number-one middleweight in the state of New Jersey.

On March 13, 1979, my twelfth fight was against a fellow by the name of Jose Pagan from Puerto Rico whose record stood at 27-83-7. He was a last-minute replacement for Ray Brayant, who had sustained a timely cut during training.

Pagan proved to be a worthy opponent. He knew all the tricks of survival while in the ring, I knocked him down twice in the first round, but he survived by tying me up every time we got close. I remember getting head-butted hard on three different occasions during this fight. His experience showed through and allowed him to last the six-round limit with me.

I won the fight on a unanimous decision. I escaped without a cut or a black eye. If I was going to get cut from a punch or, in this case, a head butt, I certainly would have in this fight. Thanks to the grace of God, I came through it unmarked.

CHAPTER 10

Overthrown

Two weeks after I won the New Jersey Middleweight Championship, the promoters from Canada flew Lou, attorney Billy DeMarcco, financial investor Freddie Brevic and me up to Montreal to work out a deal for me to fight in their country. They catered to me like I already wore the World Championship belt, and an elite group of businessmen that controlled the sport of boxing in Canada made me an offer.

First, they asked me, "Is there any reason why you're not happy with Lou's management?"

They wanted me to live and fight and to promote me out of their country.

At this point in time, Lou was treating me well. He seemed to have the right connections and picked the right fights at the right time. I really couldn't think of any reason why I might want to leave his management. I graciously and respectfully declined the offer made.

Seeing Lou later that day, I told him about the proposal made to me. Boy, did he get mad in a hurry.

"How dare these people try and steal my fighter," he said. "We're out of here. I'm leaving," he told Billy. "I want nothing to do with these people."

Billy and Fred tried to calm him down, but the effort proved futile. Lou flew back to New Jersey the very next day, leaving Billy and Freddie to work out a deal with the Canadian promoters for me.

They negotiated what I thought was a nice deal. I'd fight four times and be paid a sum of seventy thousand dollars.

Look out world, here I come! I was on my way to the big time with big money, and I planned on getting my share of it.

I fought the first of the proposed four fights in Canada on May 25, 1979, against a no-name opponent. I knocked him out in the second round with a picture-perfect right uppercut. After the fight, Lou handed me seven hundred-fifty dollars for my earnings.

"That's sure a long way from seventy thousand," I said to him.

"The amount goes up with each additional fight."

I actually made one thousand five hundred dollars, but Lou took half of everything I made. Lou acted as a promoter, manager and trainer. That it was illegal didn't faze him. He often told me, "I have the boxing commission in my back pocket so I do what I want."

I spent that summer in Ohio, enjoying my off time with my family and friends but continually training and running. The first week of August, the week of my twenty-fourth birthday, the phone rang. It was Lou, and he had information for me about my next fight.

Until then, Lou had promoted only small fight shows around the states of New York and New Jersey. All his shows were held in high schools, reception halls or at The Ice World in Totowa, New Jersey, a hockey rink with the ice covered by a thick layer of insulation and the boxing ring on the top. In addition to the seats on the two sides of the rink, chairs were placed around the ring. It held about three thousand fight fans, and was billed as "Fights on Ice." It was a big success for Lou for quite a few years.

This time, Lou wanted to venture into big-time promotions. He told me, "You're going to be one of five main events on my upcoming fight show scheduled for September 18, 1979."

When he revealed the location of his first major promotion, it surprised and impressed me. The show was to be held in Giants Stadium in the Meadowlands, New Jersey, where the New York Giants play their home football games.

"Who else will be on the fight card?" I asked.

"Scott Franks, the Heavyweight Champ of New Jersey, and Mike Rossman, the Light Heavyweight Champ of New Jersey and former Light Heavyweight Champ of the World. You will be featured as the Middleweight Champ of New Jersey, in a rematch fight with Reggie Jones."

Later, that fell through. The Jones camp refused to sign for a third fight in case he regained his title.

Lou continued, "The rest of the card will be filled out by the Welterweight Champ of New Jersey, Mike 'Nino' Gonzalez, with the Lightweight Champ of New Jersey, Gerald Hayes, fighting the 1976 Gold Medalist out of Tacoma, Washington, by the name of Rocky Lockridge."

My lease had run out in the Garrett Mountain apartment complex; so whenever I prepared for a fight in New Jersey, I stayed in a little place called the Emperor Hotel. Most people considered it a trucker's stop or a place for a one-night stand. With no swimming pool or bar or even a restaurant, small and noisy, it sat right on Route 46, running through the middle of Totowa.

I often stayed a month at a time, fought, went back to Ohio and returned again, sometimes within a week. I was there so much that I made friends with the cleaning ladies. They always cleaned my room, took my dirty, sweaty workout clothes, washed and dried them for me, folded them and returned them to my hotel room dresser. I'd always give them a tip before I returned to Ohio in appreciation for their kindness.

Arriving in camp a month in advance to start training for this big event at Giants Stadium, as I had for all of my fights so far, I asked Lou, "How much do I need to weigh at fight time?"

He said, "Between one hundred sixty-two and one hundred sixty-four pounds, just be close. Since I billed it as a non-title fight, just be close."

I said, "Good, that should be no problem. I'm at my strongest when I weigh one hundred sixty-five pounds. As a matter of fact, I'm close to that weight right now."

I unpacked my suitcases, and I had just finished neatly arranging my clothes in the dresser's drawers when the phone rang.

Lou's voice said, "I want you to drive to downtown Patterson, New Jersey. I'm holding a promotional event featuring all five state champs on my upcoming event. I billed it as the 'The Cavalcade of Champions.'"

He had arranged for a boxing ring to be set up for a publicity demonstration by all of the state champs in the town square. First, I sparred with Mike "Nino" Gonzales, predetermined to spar three rounds; but after only two rounds, Gonzalez appeared to be on Queer Street. My punching power, physical strength and overall boxing skills proved too much for a welterweight of his size and fighting ability. Gonzalez's manager, Carl Duva, Lou's older brother, made his fighter leave the ring immediately.

Carl didn't appreciate having his fighter busted up, being extremely upset with his brother Lou for suggesting the promotional match-up. Carl packed up his equipment and his fighter and left the site of the demonstration in a big hurry, visibly upset.

Since I had only sparred two rounds with Gonzalez and Mike Rossman had knocked his sparring partner out in the second round, I volunteered to put on a boxing demonstration with him. My hand speed, punch-slipping ability and quick reflexes proved to be superior to his. We sparred for three rounds, and at the end I received a fantastic ovation from the viewing crowd.

When I exited the ring, a number of his fans came up to me asking for my autograph, congratulating me on my fighting ability and swore to me, "You'll be a champ one day. You're really good."

I trained at one of two locations, either Costello's Gym in downtown Patterson or at the famed Gleason's Gym in New York City. There were so many fighters in either gym that I barely found enough room to jump rope, though there were always plenty of fighters to spar with.

Of course, I managed to spar with a few of them. I remember a light heavyweight by the name of Dave Bird. What a tough guy! He didn't have a whole lot of boxing skills, but if you ever found yourself in a gang fight, you would definitely want him on your side. He could really punch, I mean *tough*! I remember another guy, a Puerto-Rican by the name of Marciano Bernardie. I called him "the machine gun." He threw punches from bell to bell, and was always in top physical condition.

I also sparred with a real classy, intelligent, good-looking fighter, with fast hands and power to spare in either fist. He started fighting at a very young age, something like ten years old. He became a championship boxer. We fought some real exciting, competitive sparring matches. During our sparing matches, on many occasions, he felt my right uppercut on his chin. He told people in the business that I owned the best right uppercut in fight game. His name was Bobby Czyz. He went on to be one of the best boxers I ever worked out with and became the Light Heavyweight and

Cruiserweight Champ of the World.

I also worked out with an outstanding individual and an excellent fighter. I remember the first time I ever heard of him or saw him fight was against the middleweight champ of Cuba on national TV. He launched a right hand at the Cuban middleweight champ's chin, and it hit like an atom bomb. He knocked out this unquestionably tough fighter. Alex Ramos was his name, and they didn't get any better—power in both hands, always in great physical condition and always a gentleman.

Lou wanted me to have a sparring session with Alex. We hooked up at Gleason's Gym for a three-round workout. I happened to be "on" that particular day, unlike Mr. Ramos. And when the bell rang ending the second round, Alex jumped out of the ring saying, "I'm having a bad day," and never returned to complete our workout.

I trained at Gleason's Gym for the first week of my month-long preparation for the big event at Giant's Stadium. Lou would oftentimes pick me up at the hotel and drive me to the gym and back. One day as we returned from the gym, he stopped by his Teamsters office to pick up some fight flyers to post at his business friends' establishments.

After we were in his office for only a few minutes, the phone rang; Lou answered it. Exchanging only a few words with the caller, he became involved in a heated argument. I overheard every word of the conversation, so I knew it concerned ticket sales for the upcoming show.

When Lou hung up the phone, he immediately began pacing quickly around his office. The whole time he was pacing, he was scratching his head and repeating over and over, "Tickets aren't selling, tickets aren't selling. What am I going to do? I'm going to lose my ass! What am I going to do?"

Realizing he was stressed, I asked, "What's up? What's

wrong?"

"Though five New Jersey State Champs will be on the card," he confided, "I don't have a fight strong enough to draw fifteen thousand fight fans to the stadium, the amount of ticket sells I need to generate so I make money. I have to pay people back the money they've loaned me. I used their money for the promotion of the show. I don't want to end up in the East River wearing cement shoes."

Lou was overweight; and, seeing him so upset about the phone call, I worried that, in his stressed state, he might have a heart attack.

I tried to comfort him by saying, "Don't worry, it'll work out for you somehow."

Approximately two and half weeks from fight time, Lou told me, "I'm changing your training site from Gleason's Gym to a millionaire's estate in Hopewell, New Jersey."

"Why?"

"It will be a better place to train."

Lou being my manager, part-time trainer and—at least so I thought—a friend, the guy who was going to guide me to a world boxing championship title, my destiny, I found no reason to question or doubt anything he told me or asked of me. Like a child who has heard the song of the Pied Piper, I listened and followed. If Lou had told me to jump in a lake three times a day, that it would help me achieve my destiny of being world middleweight champ, believe me, I'd have been going for a swim three times a day.

The training facility I was about to use belonged to a man by the name of John Zuccarrelli from Hopewell. He accumulated his wealth by owning a large number of garbage trucks and securing the contracts to service the entire southern region of New Jersey. His estate reminded me of another mansion I visited during my amateur boxing career.

In 1977, I had experienced the extreme pleasure and

great honor of touring Graceland, Elvis Presley's estate. The USA Boxing Team, which I by then belonged to though I didn't fight on this occasion, received an invitation to tour Graceland while in Memphis, Tennessee.

A big, beautiful tour bus drove both boxing teams. It pulled into Graceland through the front gate and right up to the front door of Elvis's mansion. As the fighters got out of the bus, the *ABC Wide World of Sports* TV cameras filmed the event.

The cameraman zoomed in on one of the USA fighters for a close-up shot, so I had the great honor of appearing on national TV on the *Wide World of Sports*.

After our tour of Graceland was complete, the bus driver took us to an amusement park located nearby. Our tour guide told us "When Elvis lived, on a Friday or Saturday night, after the park closed for the day he rented the entire park. He paid all of the employees to stay and let his daughter ride rides, play games, eat cotton candy and enjoy the fun and excitement of an amusement park. This way he could have some quality time with his daughter and not be swamped by fans asking for autographs."

While we were walking around the park, our tour guide directed us to a little theater. The fighters were escorted in and seated in the first two rows. A group of imitation New York Rockettes appeared on stage and proceeded to put on a beautifully choreographed dance routine to music.

In the middle of their routine, one the Rockettes stopped dancing and began pacing up and down the stage, looking at the group of fighters and coaches sitting before her. Looking at all very intensely, she stopped and pointed her finger directly at me, summoning me to join her and the rest of the dancers on stage.

I got out of my seat and walked up the steps leading to the stage. When I reached the top step, she took me by my hand, led me right to the middle of the dancers and inserted me into the dance line. I proceeded to kick my legs up and down trying my best to simulate their movements. It sure beat being in the ring getting my face hit, if you know what I mean.

For a guy who collected other people's garbage, Mr. Zuccarrelli did very well for himself. He enjoyed boxing and had constructed a building on his property. Inside this building he put up a boxing ring, heavy bag, speed bag rack, shower, sauna, bathroom, kitchen, TV—all the luxuries of home.

He did enjoy his privacy, though. He'd built his mansion out in the country on a big estate. The distance from the main road to his mansion was at least a quarter of a mile, and the driveway was made completely of concrete. He also owned a stable full of horses; and every morning when I ran, a beautiful Arabian grazed out in the pasture.

When I was growing up, my father owned a couple of horses; and I knew horses loved to eat apples, especially a fresh-picked apple from the tree. A big old apple tree grew near the front gate. Every morning I fed the Arabian an apple from it once I finished my run. When I left for my run, he would be grazing out in the middle of the pasture. By the time I finished, I would find him standing near the front gate, right next to the driveway, making it impossible for me not to see him, waiting for me to feed him an apple.

At first, I was impressed and excited about the new environment that Lou had forced on me to train in. Then, Lou told me, "Tomorrow Scott's going to join you until fight time."

Scott acted as Lou's second pair of eyes. He reported everything back to Lou—especially if I didn't follow Lou's directives to the letter. I did nothing wrong, always following Lou's orders to the best of my ability. I believed in him; and besides, I was hundreds of miles away from family and friends, totally isolated from everyone I knew or trusted. I really had no other choice but to trust Lou.

Lou needed to travel two and a half hours each way to bring us sparring partners and food. The trip being so long, sparring partners didn't enjoy or want to make the long drive daily. When he could find sparring partners for me, they always seemed to be light heavyweights with slow hand speed and hardly any foot movement. In a ten-day period before the fight, I only sparred a total of three times. Normally, I sparred six days per week, right up until the day before fight day.

Things didn't feel right to me deep down in my soul. Though I did believe in Lou and trusted him completely, something just wasn't right.

CHAPTER 11

Changes

Five days away from the big show; and though I hadn't sparred like I usually did in preparation for a fight, I was still in great physical condition. I was running every morning—my knee had long since healed—resting all day, taking a walk in the afternoon just to loosen up until time to train in the gym.

That day, as I ended my training, Lou pulled up on me and asked me how much I weighed.

"There's a scale, let's see."

I got on the scale, and it read one hundred sixty-six pounds—two pounds over the weight limit he'd set for me four weeks earlier.

"Two pounds in five days," I told Lou, "is not a problem."

Lou then informed me that he'd changed the contract.

"What do you mean?" I asked.

His exact words were, "I need you to fight Mike 'Nino' Gonzalez, and you have to weigh one hundred fifty-five pounds or you're not fighting."

"That's eleven pounds in five days," I protested. "I'm already in great shape. I have no more than two pounds I can afford to lose."

"Trust me and believe in me," Lou said. "I've been around the fight game a lot longer than you have. I know what I'm doing."

Being young, naive, too trusting—or just plan stupid—I again followed his directive, as I always did. He put me on a strict diet, a diet of lettuce. Lou allowed me to eat one bowl of lettuce a day for five days, without any tomatoes, carrots or dressing—just dry lettuce. Each afternoon following our training session, he took Scott and me out to eat, since there wasn't any food at our training/living facility. During our daily supper, Lou ordered me a bowl of dry lettuce, and that was it.

He also instructed me to take laxatives he supplied to me twice a day, once in the morning and once in the evening.

"Continue doing your roadwork in the morning and training in the gym," he said.

I obeyed. Lou informed me that it took some persuading, but I would make the weigh-ins the day before the fight instead of the customary same day. This would give me a chance to put back on some of the weight and strength I'd lost.

Though it didn't sound or feel right to me, I ate lettuce and drank the least amount of water possible for five days. I believed in and trusted Lou blindly. I felt confident that, putting his experience together with my ability, I would realize my destiny of Middleweight Champ of the World.

When it came time to weigh in the day before the fight, I walked into the room designated as the weigh-in room at Giants Stadium.

Scott Franks's opponent, Bill Connell, the first person to speak to me, said, "My God, Rusty, what did he do to you? You look sick—no, you look like death warmed over. Man, be careful, he's trying to get you hurt."

With thoughts of the upcoming fight running through

my head, I just blew off his comments and continued to walk towards the scale. I took off all my clothes and stepped onto the scale.

The official said, "Rosenberger, one hundred fifty-five." I had lost eleven pounds in five days.

Nino Gonzalez got on the scale, and the official called out, "Gonzalez, one hundred fifty-five."

His normal weight was one hundred forty-seven pounds, meaning he had put on eight pounds of muscle while Lou made me melt eleven pounds of muscle off my well-built, well-conditioned body in a five-day period of time.

The day of the big show at Giants Stadium was September 18, 1979; and my father, Ray, amateur trainer Bob, brother-in-law George and a friend, Mark, flew to New Jersey to be at the fight and cheer me on. They flew into Newark Airport, where I agreed to pick them up on their arrival. They wanted to spend the day with me up until fight time.

At the airport, I found the gate they would be arriving at. I got there a few minutes early so I wouldn't miss them. I was standing at the bottom of the off-ramp waiting for them to deplane and walk down. I was standing in broad daylight; and I saw my father, trainer and two close friends walking towards me, only they didn't stop to greet me. They continued to walk right past me.

"Hey, guys, where are you going?" I called.

They stopped, turned around and, looking at me in surprise, said, "Rusty, is that you? What's wrong with you? Why are you so skinny? Are you sick?"

I had lost so much weight even my family and friends didn't recognize me.

From the time they arrived in New Jersey until fight time was only about three hours. I suggested that we eat then so the food would have enough time to digest before my fight. I drove to a restaurant on Route 46 in Totowa called Mr. Anthony's. While we were seated at a large round table, right after the waitress took our orders, Lou walked in. He greeted everyone with a big smile and welcomed my guests. Then, he held out his hand. I put out mine to accept two little white pills.

"What are these pills for, Lou?" I asked.

"In case you're cut in the fight tonight, these pills will help clot your blood, stop you from bleeding so the referee won't stop the fight. Make sure you take these pills an hour before you're ready to go on to fight."

After dinner, we all returned to my home away from home, my hotel room, to rest until fight time. I gave the two pills to my father to hold. I rested for about an hour, and then the phone rang. My father answered. Lou advised us to get ready and come to Giants Stadium.

Before my dad hung up the phone, I heard him say to Lou, "OK, I'll make sure he takes them."

When we walked into Giants Stadium, with thousands of people everywhere and me concentrating on my upcoming fight, I ran directly into Ray "Boom Boom" Mancini. He told me he had just signed a pro contract with new manager Dave Wolfe, who also wrote sports for the *New York Times*.

Boom-Boom and I are friends. We fought together at the same time, fighting out of Youngstown, Ohio. We often trained in the same gym. He asked me to show him around Giants Stadium and introduce him to some of the other fighters.

"Rusty, you look like you've lost a lot of weight since the last time I saw you," he said.

I told him of the last-minute weight limit restriction and of Lou's special diet.

"How do you feel?" he asked.

"Weak," I said.

I took Boom-Boom on a tour of Giants Stadium,

introducing him to some of the fighters that would be fighting this evening; I even introduced Boom-Boom to Lou.

My father approached and said to me, "You'll be fighting in about an hour, you better take these two pills Lou gave you."

That was when I made the biggest mistake of my life. I took the two small white pills in my hand, opened my mouth, laid them as far back on my tongue as possible and swallowed them, just as my manager, Lou Duva, had instructed me to do.

CHAPTER 12

The Long Fall

It was fight time at Giants Stadium, and the arena was packed. I had taken those blood-clotting pills, as Lou had directed me to do. I don't remember much after the pills entered my system.

From what my trainer Bob told me, I was dressed, ready to go on and fight, sitting in a chair. Instead of loosening up as I had done for all of my amateur and professional fights, Bob told me I sat down on a chair that had been placed in the runway of the stadium, the runway being the access to and from the field that the football players used. He said I feel asleep sitting there in that chair.

I don't remember it. Those must have been some strong blood-clotting pills he gave me. Then, it was my turn to fight. From what Bob tells me, Lou grabbed me by my shoulder, shook me and said, "Come on, let's go."

I was escorted to the ring, where I fought, or gave a reasonable facsimile of fighting, a ten-round fight, losing in a unanimous decision. I only remember bits and pieces after taking those mysterious blood-clotting pills.

I don't remember much from the next couple of days, either. Bob tells me he and I went to Lou's office the day after the fight to collect my earnings. The first words out of Lou's mouth, according to Bob were, "Don't worry about the loss to Nino last night. We'll fight him again at Ice World, and you'll knock him out. Just don't worry about it."

It came out later that Lou had arranged for Nino and me to fight in a last-minute decision. The bookies who had put odds on the betting circle were unaware I had lost eleven pounds in five days. They thought I would weigh in at my normal 164 pounds, and Nino would be coming up to 164. Since that was my natural weight while Nino wouldn't be used to carrying the extra, the bookies had me a 7-3 favorite to win the fight.

Since Nino had won at Giants Stadium, Lou was planning a rematch at The Ice World. The bookies would make Nino the favorite this time, and Lou knew I'd knock him out. Guess who Lou was going to be betting on this time.

The day after I fought Nino at Giants Stadium, I drove my father, my trainer Bob and two friends all the way back to Ohio in my car. It wasn't until three days after the fight when, sitting at my mother's kitchen table, I looked up and asked my father, "What happened?"

"What do you mean, 'what happened?'" he said with a smile.

"I mean, in the fight, what happened? Who won? How did I get here, how did I get back to Ohio?"

I had no memory of those three days whatsoever. I did everything on reflex. God had walked hand-in-hand with me—talking, eating, driving and maybe even breathing for me. It had to be God. I don't remember a thing.

On the fourth day following the fight, I began to feel a gnawing pain in my head. By the fifth day, the pain was unbearable. I actually cried like a baby, tears and all. My head was in incredible pain every time I took a step, coughed or sneezed. Why?

I experience pain like I've never, ever, felt before in my life. After I took a bottle of extra-strength aspirin that didn't ease the pain, my father convinced me to go to the hospital.

He took me to the Trumbull Memorial Hospital in Warren, Ohio. We entered the emergency room, where the attending physician assessed my condition. He immediately called Dr. Ready, a neurologist, on his pager to summon him to the hospital. Upon Dr. Ready's arrival, he ordered a CAT scan.

The nurses put me on a gurney and wheeled me into the hallway, placing me just outside the door leading into the CAT scan room. I lay there for a period of time as they readied the room for my test. I remember lying there, feeling exhausted, with my head pounding like it was about to explode. I closed my eyes and tried to rest.

The next thing I remember is seeing a very, very bright light in front of my eyes, as if someone had turned on a spotlight right in my face. Everything in front of me was a blur. I focused my eyes.

What I saw was a miracle. It was a man with long hair, wearing a white robe, sitting in a chair. I was flying at warp speed; and, as I got closer, I could make out his face. It was the face of God. I got within inches of Him, and he spoke to me.

"It's not your time," he said.

I immediately opened my eyes. Moments later, I was wheeled into the CAT scan room where the test was done. It felt to me as if I had been on a trip for a long, long time.

I was then taken up to a room in the hospital to wait for the test results to be sent to Dr. Ready. A short time later, the doctor appeared in my doorway with a very concerned look on his face.

"I can't believe you're not dead, or in a coma," he said.

"Our brains float in a fluid called the cerebral fluid. This fluid acts as a shock absorber so our brains will not bounce in our skull as we go through our daily routine of walking, running, jumping or, in your case, boxing.

"All the fluid in your brain has been knocked out. There is no fluid cushioning your brain at the present time. Your brain is swollen, pressing against your skull. That's why you're in so much pain. Rusty, you're a lucky man. If you had received any more trauma to your head, your brain would have had no more room to expand. It would have burst, and you'd be dead."

With time and a steroid medication, my brain was reduced back to its normal size.

I had lost fights before, but never anything like this. It confused and angered me. I kept asking myself, "What just happened to me?"

I was totally confused. I couldn't stop wondering why Lou did what he did to me. Something way back in the depths of my mind kept asking, "Did he set you up for a fall?" I kept telling myself, "He wouldn't want me to lose, would he?"

Something just wasn't right about the whole ordeal. Why would he want his fighter to lose weight in such a hurry? Anyone involved with sports knows that losing that amount of weight in the short time span allotted me was only going to make me weak. As far as those so-called blood-clotting pills…

First, no pill in 2002, the year I wrote this book, will clot my blood in one hour's time, so what were those pills he made me take in 1979?

Second, I had fought fifty-five amateur fights and fourteen pro fights and never had a cut or a bloody nose. So, why did he suddenly start worrying about me cutting and bleeding?

To this day I ask myself, "Why."

I wrote earlier that a fighter has to be able to trust his manager completely. Well, I couldn't do that anymore. I felt betrayed, and I couldn't fight if I felt that way. I decided to leave Lou's management.

I went back to my old gym and was training there giving my future in the boxing game some serious thought. I couldn't trust Lou to manage me any longer, but I still wanted to fight. I needed to fight; I had something I had to prove to the world and to myself. I figured that finding a new manager would be easy. I had a record of fourteen wins and one loss with eight knockouts.

My first thought was to call on Blackie Gennaro, Earnie Shavers' manager. He was from Youngstown. and he had seen me fight on many occasions plus I knew him personally. I contacted Blackie and told him of the underhanded treatment I had received from Lou, and he agreed to take me on as my manager.

However, before he could sign me to a contract, I had to be free and clear from the contract I had with Lou Duva.

Blackie called Lou to first ask if he had any problem with me going to South Africa to fight on a fight card featuring South African Gerrie Coetzee and Mike Koranicki, to be held in Johannesburg's Rand Stadium. I had been sparring with big Mike for about a month in preparation for his upcoming fight over in South Africa.

"Rusty is still under contract with me," Lou said. "If you take him, I'll see you in court."

"Would you be willing to sell Rusty's contract?" Blackie asked.

"Ten thousand dollars."

"Okay, I can agree to that if you can take it as a percentage out of the fighter's pay until the full amount is reached."

"No, no deal," said Lou. He hung up the phone.

My boxing career came to a standstill, though I

continued to train.

A friend I had gone to school with had been boxing for a period of time and was involved with Don King—actually, more with King's son, Carl. His name was Sterling "Pookie" McPherson. He was a great guy with the gift of gab, and he did have some boxing skills. The biggest problem he had was a lack of self-confidence. He never believed he was as good as he was, and he was good.

He made friends with Mike Dokes while he trained at the Kings' training camp in Orwell, Ohio. He even became Dokes's manager for a time, booking him on national TV.

Under his management, Carl had a middleweight who was knocking out and busting up all his sparring partners. "Pookie," as we called him, convinced Carl that I could give his guy some real work. His name was Dwight Davidson.

I can remember sparring with him prior to a fight he had scheduled to be telecast on national TV. Sure enough, I gave him all he could handle and a little bit more. One week before the fight, we were sparring; and I hit him with a vicious right hand to the body, bruising his ribs. The show had to be rescheduled so his ribs had enough time to heal.

Something was happening to me, though, and I didn't understand why. I was getting hit with so many punches. Before the gruesome beating I took in Giants Stadium, my slip game was outstanding. It was almost impossible to land a clean punch on me. Afterward, I kept getting nailed.

Why? I was in great shape, as always, and I was more motivated than ever. I didn't understand what had happened to my boxing ability.

While I was at the Kings' training camp, I ended up sparring with Larry Holmes's younger brother, Mark. He was very fast-handed. We sparred all week, and he told me that I was the best sparring partner he'd ever had. He asked if I would be interested in coming to Easton, Pennsylvania, to spar with him. I agreed; and soon after, I was flown to Easton and put up in a nice hotel for a month.

During that time, Sugar Ray Leonard and Tommy Hearns fought on national TV for the first time. The fight was held in Las Vegas, Nevada. Larry Holmes was a great fighter. Unfortunately, he fought in the shadows of the greatest of all time, Muhammad Ali.

One day while I was training, Larry came in the gym and started hitting his heavy bag. No, I mean his *heavy* bag. It had to weigh at least two hundred pounds. It was the biggest heavy bag I've ever seen. I could barely move it when I punched with all the power I had—and my boxing record speaks for the kind of power I have. It hung down from the ceiling on an eight-foot-long chain.

He started dancing in the same spot. At the same time, he started swinging this huge heavy bag back and forth. He made this bag swing so fast that it was actually making a whooshing noise as it swung past him.

All of a sudden, he stepped in front of this swinging bag and delivered a left jab that looked like a piston on a Navy battleship. It was so fast that I could barely see it; but when that jab hit that huge heavy bag, the bag bounced up in the air and stopped dead. It didn't move. It made me cringe at the thought of ever having one of those jabs hit me. I'd rather be kicked by a mule.

Larry's house was beautiful. It had an enclosed swimming pool. On a nice day, he could push a button and the ceiling would open up to let the sun shine in. You know those black-faced stone jockey figures holding lanterns in people's front yards? Well, Larry had one, also. Only the face on his was painted white. When you're the heavyweight champ of the world, not too many people will say anything about it to you, know what I mean?

He owned a bar/restaurant where, after the workouts, all

the sparring partners would go and eat. One day, we were sitting there eating, and a commercial came on TV advertising a new line of car by Datsun, the Datsun Z/X. When the commercial was over, all Larry said was, "I likes those cars."

The very next day, we were eating our dinner when, outside the bar, we heard the sound of tires screeching. We looked out in front. There was Larry, crawling out of a brand new Datsun Z/X.

He says, "I told you I likes those cars."

Must be nice!

It shouldn't have surprised me, though, after I saw his ten-car garage. He had every expensive car there that I could think of. There was a Rolls-Royce, a Jaguar, a Corvette and a Cadillac, just to name a few. It was the first time I'd ever seen that many expensive cars under one roof. It was very impressive, and I knew I possessed that kind of talent, and I wanted to live the way he lived.

Larry flew out to Vegas to watch the Leonard versus Hearns fight in person. Before he left, he invited all the sparring partners over to his home to watch the fight on his big screen TV. He had a satellite dish that picked up any televised program there was.

Four of us sat in Larry Holmes's basement watching the fight show. Between rounds, the TV camera scanned the audience at ringside. The cameraman spotted Larry Holmes, and the announcer told the worldwide audience, "There's Larry Holmes, the Heavyweight Champ of the World."

We immediately looked at his wife to get her response. She smiled ear to ear, and said, "That's my man."

That showed me how much she cared and the pride she carried inside of her for him. That's what I wanted to happen to my life.

Upon his return from Las Vegas, Larry was at the gym

watching his brother Mark preparing for a sparring session. He told us, "If any one of you sparring partners can knock Mark down, I'll pay you an extra one hundred dollars."

During that workout, almost every jab Mark threw at me hit me. I couldn't see them coming at me any more. I had lost my slip game.

I turned up the intensity level and threw a bone-crushing right hand that caught him high on his head and tore his headgear completely off, leaving him wobbling but not down. Larry told me, that, though I didn't knock him down, "that was a hell of a right hand." I received fifty dollars for my efforts.

Larry Holmes is a first-class human being, and one of the best heavyweight champs in the history of the game. It was an extreme pleasure and honor to be that "up close and personal" with a man of his athletic ability and class. Thank you for the experience and memories, Mr. Holmes.

The thoughts of Larry Holmes's setup in Easton left me wanting to fight badly. That really left me no choice. If I wanted to fight, Lou Duva was the only man who could be my manager. I didn't like it, but I went back to him.

CHAPTER 13

One More Try

Lou made arrangements for me to start training again in New Jersey. When I first returned to the gym, he arranged for me spar Bobby Czyz. Bobby was getting ready for a televised fight card out of Tampa, Florida. I was supposed to go to Florida for a month of fun in the sun—after I trained, of course.

Lou assigned a Puerto-Rican guy as my trainer/watchdog. When Bobby and I sparred, my right hand found its mark, time and time again. My watchdog kept warning me, "If Lou sees you hit Bobby with that right hand, he's going to stop you from sparring and you won't go to Florida with us."

Bobby was a world-class boxer with fast hands, power and stamina—not one to take lightly. With my eyes not telling me when punches were coming like they used to, and fighting against a fighter with excellent boxing skills, I needed to fight him hard. Either that or get beat up on a daily basis.

As my luck would have it, Lou showed up at the gym unannounced one day while Czyz and I were in the ring sparring. I hit Bobby more times than Lou must have cared to see. He sent me home. I missed another free vacation and a chance to reach my destiny.

While I was back home in Ohio, Larry Ringler, who was the *Warren Tribune Chronicle* sports editor, and I talked on the phone. He informed me he'd sent Lou a copy of the article he'd published shortly after the Giants Stadium ordeal. The article told of my thoughts of how Lou done me wrong and the underhanded tactics he used on me leading up to the Giants Stadium fight show. The article also included the neurologist's report from the hospital that told of the damage my brain had suffered.

"When did you send him this copy?" I asked.

"Last week," he said.

The following week, Lou told me he had lined me up to fight a proven tough guy. His jaw might as well have been made out of steel, and he could punch like a jackhammer. His name was Joe Tiabari.

I left the next week, a month in advance per usual, arrived safely in New Jersey and got settled in at my home away from home, the Emperor Hotel. My training was going well, except I was being hit with punches that normally I'd slip or dance out of punching range. I was getting hit with hard punches that should never have come near me. Something was wrong. It was all different.

The day before my fight with Tiabari, Lou had arranged a sparring session with Christy Elliot at his brother Carl's gym in downtown Patterson, in that ten-by-ten puncher's ring I mentioned earlier. Christy Elliot was a hard-punching light heavyweight when he was in his prime, but he hadn't fought in years.

I was asking myself why Lou wanted me to spar this hard-punching, out-of-shape retired boxer the day before my fight. Normally, a fighter doesn't spar the day before a fight. As we entered the ring, I spoke to Christy, and he had not one word to say to me in return. He wore this intense glare in his eyes, as though he wanted to hurt me real bad, as though he were on a mission.

The bell rang, and he flew across the ring after me. I out-boxed him the first round with relative ease. He was already beginning to get winded. In the second round, he trapped me on the ropes. I had gotten too relaxed and my intensity level was diminished—after all, I thought, he's not the same fighter as when he was in his prime.

He still could punch with dynamite in either hand, though. He unleashed a right hand on the tip of my chin. The next thing I remember is coming back to consciousness after doing a nosedive onto the canvas floor. He hit me so hard, so viciously, that, believe it or not, my head didn't hurt; my toes—that's right, my toes—hurt.

The next day I was fighting an eight-round fight against another power puncher. This fight once again left me wondering about Lou Duva and his managerial tactics.

Tiaberi was billed as a knockout artist from Vineland, New Jersey. The fight proved to be a hard one for me. He punched like a ton of rocks had somehow found their way to the inside of his gloves. Even so, I was winning the fight when he landed a hard body shot, bruising my ribs. I lost my breath and my ability to move away from trouble.

From then on, he pounded me. He hit me with punches that I should have slipped easily, but they connected—connected hard. He won an eight-round split decision.

Between Christy Elliot introducing me to the canvas and then Tiaberi hitting my head like a kid trying to break open a piñata, the next day my head wound up in trouble again. Things didn't feel right. That beating I endured at Giants Stadium changed my fighting ability drastically, for the worse.

The whole situation reinforced my distrust of Lou, and again I left his management. This time, I turned over my boxing career and future in the ring to Bob Miketa. Bob was my amateur trainer and a friend, someone I knew I could trust.

Miketa scheduled a fight card to be held on April 30, 1980. The fight card was held at my old stomping grounds, the Struthers Fieldhouse. My opponent was Bennie Mitchell from Columbus, who was tall and thin. In the second round, I had Bennie against the ropes, his hands high up around his head. I stepped in and landed a hard right-handed body shot to his solar plexus. I immediately followed up with a left upper cut to his body.

When I landed the right, he bent forward from the effect of the hard body shot. As he bent his upper body forward and I threw the left upper cut, his elbow and my left biceps muscle made contact. I felt a burning pain in my left biceps, like someone had set it on fire. Unable to continue, I threw in the towel, losing my third fight in as many outings.

My left biceps was damaged. I had no strength. I went to a chiropractor, a family doctor, but got no explanation of the damage that had been done. I finally went to a doctor a friend suggested to me, Dr. Deliquadrae in Girard, Ohio. He referred me to a specialist in the Cleveland Clinic. X-ray results showed that my entire biceps muscle was torn off the tendon.

I was scheduled for surgery at the Cleveland Clinic to have my biceps muscle reattached to my tendon. The surgery was performed by Dr. Bergfield and was successful. Though I had a scar on my arm and the muscle was shorter in length than my right biceps, the arm worked again.

I still wanted to be a champ. When you've gotten so close to the big time and then had someone you were supposed to be able to trust rip it from your heart, it's a hard pill to swallow. Hardest of all was to let go and admit that my destiny, becoming a world middleweight champ, was never to be.

During my private moments I often thought about the injustice I felt Lou Duva had done to me. I even went as far as thinking crazy. His office in Totowa was inside a two-story building with no windows, all made of brick. There was only one door at the top of the stairs to let you access his top floor offices. I'd think about traveling to New Jersey, going to his office, making all the employees leave the building and holding him hostage until the news media came to cover the event. With the TV cameras rolling, I fantasized about making him tell the whole world what he had done to me.

Then I thought, no, I'd get arrested or get shot. It wouldn't be worth it. *I'll make him stand up for his actions somehow, some way. If all else fails, eventually, he'll have to face God for his criminal acts. One way or another, he won't get away with it.*

In my mind, I hadn't been defeated, at least by my standards. I still had a yearning for greatness. I wanted to be the best in the world. But as time slipped by, day after day, week after week, month after month, year after year, my dream also slipped away.

I fought a few more times, but it was futile, I was getting hit with punches I didn't even see coming. I fought on July 24, 1982, in Niles, Ohio, at a disco called The VIP. It was a real classy nightclub, and they had erected the ring in the middle of the dance floor. I was fighting a tough guy out of the Columbus area. During the first round of our eight-round contest, I got hit with almost every punch this guy was throwing at me.

"Why?" I asked myself. "What's going on?"

In the second round, I saw the man coming at me with fists flying like he was shooting a Gatling gun. I saw four gloves. I was seeing double.

I closed my right eye so I was able to see only one set of

gloves coming at me. This helped me during the fight, and I was able to win a close decision.

Ray "Boom-Boom" Mancini fought the same night, only he fought in Warren at the Mollenkoff Stadium against Ernesto Espana, defending his lightweight title.

A short time later I was driving down a freeway at night; and as the oncoming cars approached, I saw four headlights coming at me instead of two. I'd be watching TV and see two pictures in front of me. I'd try reading; and, unless I closed one of my eyes, it was impossible. My depth perception was gone. Everything looked flat, and my peripheral vision had vanished.

I started to understand why I was being hit so easily. I couldn't determine where the punches were coming from. Since the fight at Giants Stadium, it had gotten progressively worse, I finally figured it out. During my fight against Gonzalez, not only did my brain suffer damage but a muscle in my eye must have also been damaged.

I had an eye exam; and sure enough, the muscle that moves my right eye left or right was torn. The doctor first prescribed glasses that had a strong prism in them. The prism would turn my right eye in alignment with the left eye so I would see just one object in front of me. That was okay for a while, until that burning desire to be a world champ hit me again. How could I fight with glasses on?

As time passed, I resigned myself a little more each day to the fact that my destiny of ever becoming a world middleweight champ would never be realized. I felt like a loser. What woman is ever going to want an old, broken-down boxer who talks funny and walks funny? Is there a God? Why has He done this to a man who used to pray to him every day while training to be a world champ? Why would God let a man like Lou get away with a travesty like this? Why?

CHAPTER 14

Moving Slowly On

One winter's night in January of 1982 I was at home when the phone rang. A friend of mine asked me if I wanted to go out and have some fun at a local bar.

My first response was, "No, I just got done working out. I'm going to take a shower and watch some TV tonight."

"I just broke up with my girlfriend," he said, "and could use some company."

I relented and said that I would go out with him. We ended up in a nightclub.

As we walked into the club, I noticed that it had once been a movie theater. The bar was up near the front where the concession stand once stood, and the dance floor was down where the theater's screen had hung.

The club was dark; it took a while for my eyes to adjust—as best they could. After they did, I looked down at the dance floor and saw a girl dancing slowly with a guy. Maybe it was a trick of the lighting, but the air around this girl's head seemed to glow, like a halo. I immediately walked down to the dance floor and right up to her. I put my hand on the guy's chest and pushed him back. Looked closely at this beautiful young lady, I asked her if she'd care to dance with me.

She took a step back, looked me up and down and said, "Okay."

We started dancing that night, and I instantly fell in love with her. She was young, only seventeen years old to my twenty-six, but we fell in love. Soon, we became inseparable.

Her name was Cindy Adams, and she's still the prettiest girl I've ever seen. Now, for the last twenty years, it's been Cindy Rosenberger.

I made Cindy a promise that before ending my days in the ring I'd make enough money fighting to build her a big, beautiful house to raise our family in.

The year that I met her was the year she graduated from high school. Cindy gave us our first beautiful boy on September 24, 1983. We named him Scott Russell Rosenberger.

My brother-in-law, George, a deputy sheriff for Trumbull County, helped get me a job as a correction officer working inside the county lockup. I worked there for almost a year until budget cuts forced them to lay me off. All the while, I constantly had friends asking me to teach them boxing moves.

I started training people; and, for the ones that stayed consistent, I began to see a change in their physiques. The workout that I devised caused them to burn off fat and lose weight. They built muscle, their self-confidence level increased, it relieved their pent up stress and, best of all, the whole time they were having fun doing it.

One day, one of my clients said to me, "Rusty, that's a good idea you have, teaching people boxing moves and getting exercise all at the same time."

When he said that, a light went off in my head. Boxing and exercise. "Boxercise."

One of my clients was an old boxing friend by the name

of Greg Augustine. He was a good fighter with extra-fast hands and could really punch, for a lightweight. He'd gotten away from boxing competitively and pursued the promotional end of the game. Whenever someone put on a fight show anywhere in the USA and the promoter of the show needed to have an opponent to fill up his fight card, they'd get a hold of Greg; and he would find them the kind of opponent to fit that spot.

At this time I was still trying to fulfill my destiny. I wasn't ready to admit defeat, not yet. I vowed to myself never to quit. So, I became a constant pain in the ass to Greg. I'd call him every day, asking him to line me up a fight somewhere, anywhere.

He finally got me a fight in Atlantic City against a real rugged guy by the name of Henry Milligan. An eight-round fight, televised live on ESPN's Thursday night fights— though I had not fought for a long period of time and was doing anything I could to find a job to support my growing family.

I'd already promised Cindy I'd build her a house. That September, I also had a baby boy to take care of and raise. My time was running out, and I knew it. I had to win that fight on national-worldwide TV. I was thinking, *If I can look impressive, I could be on my way once again.*

Just my luck, I came down with a bad cold the week before the fight; I couldn't run or train all week. Still, I made it to the ring. This would be my last opportunity to show my stuff, and I knew it.

I won the first two rounds, out-boxing him with my foot speed and combinations. In the third round, with one minute remaining, I hit him with a left hook that almost tore his head off his shoulders. He didn't go down, but he was visibly shaken.

The fourth round, he started to land some hard body shots. Milligan was strong and could really punch, hard. I was still moving well on my feet, though, and able to stay out of harm's way.

Midway through the fifth round I threw a right hand that missed its mark, but I followed up with a picture-perfect left hook, cutting him over his right eye. He became enraged. He felt like a grizzly bear might have felt, powerful, and I was getting tired.

He then landed a crushing right hand to my head that I never saw coming

As I tired, I lost control of my bad eye. By the fifth round, it would sometimes drift completely to the righthand corner of my eyesocket. I saw two of everything. He trapped me on the ropes and banged punches off my face and body. I came back towards the end of the round by landing a beautiful right uppercut followed by a left hook, which got his attention. He held on.

This is what is called "war games." I fought him as long and as hard as my conditioning would allow me, and he did his absolute best, too. I had better techniques, but unfortunately, his conditioning and perfect eyesight did me in.

In the seventh round, he trapped me against the ropes again and banged away, as though I were a punching bag, until the referee stepped in and gave me a standing eight count. He asked me if I wanted to continue. I nodded my head yes.

Henry, with his left eye cut and bleeding, moved in for the kill. He nailed me with another right hand and a left hook, knocking me halfway through the ropes. Down I went. When the referee asked me again if I wanted to go on, I sadly, but wisely said "no," lowered my head and walked back to my corner.

While sitting in my corner, catching my breath, I saw the TV cameraman focusing in on Bob and me. I yelled loud enough so my wife, watching back home could hear,

"Sorry, Cindy."

Again, my dream of fulfilling my destiny as world middleweight champ was put on hold. I still wasn't ready to quit.

One month later, the phone rang. It was Greg. He asked me, "Would you be interested in fighting in Atlantic City?"

"I'm in decent shape," I responded, "but not fighting shape. When's this fight taking place?"

"Tomorrow night," he told me, "and you'll be fighting the number-seven ranked light heavyweight in the world, James McDonald."

Cindy and I had had two more children by this time, both boys. To our despair, they both passed away. Our second child, Steve, was born with hypoplastic left heart syndrome, which affects one out of every twelve thousand children born. He died on the operating table during open-heart surgery when he was only five days old.

Our thirdborn boy, whom we named Tony, was diagnosed with neuroblastoma, which affects one out of every one hundred thousand children born, when he was one and a half years old. After many operations, chemotherapy and radiation treatments, he died of cancer at the age of two and a half years in my wife's arms in our mobile home.

The poor baby suffered with cancer for eleven months after being diagnosed. He was admitted to the Akron Children's Hospital, where my wife and I spent all of our time. We wanted to be close to our dying child. "Tone-tone" we often called him.

He was a special boy. The entire time he fought this fatal disease, he never cried or gave us any of the kind of problem you expect out of a two-year-old. My wife and I spent as much time with our dying child as we possibly could. During this trying time in our lives we were forced to live on welfare.

Though I wasn't in fighting shape, I took the fight on one day's notice. Where else was I going to make two thousand dollars? In our financial condition, we needed the money.

I was flown from Youngstown Municipal Airport to Philadelphia Airport; then, I was driven to Atlantic City in a stretch limousine. The beautiful gold limousine pulled up to the front of the hotel. The driver opened the door for me to exit; and for just a split second, everyone there stopped and looked to see who it was getting out of the limousine. What a great feeling it was—like I was someone really special.

A thought ran through my mind: if I hadn't gotten hurt, I'd have had this feeling for real.

Back to reality. The fight was scheduled for ten rounds. I was in it. During the first round, I moved on my feet well and stayed out of the way. When I got to my corner between rounds, a makeshift trainer said, "Throw your right hand, he's wide open for it, throw your right hand."

The bell rang for the second round. I was moving on my feet, dancing the boxer's two-step, until for some unknown reason I stopped and lay against the ropes. McDonald must have heard my corner telling me to throw the right hand, because he threw his. I never saw it coming.

He launched a right hand loaded with an atom bomb that exploded on my forehead, knocking me down. When he hit me, the actual time of the glove hitting my forehead was but a split second. It was so weird—as I was being hit, I can remember saying to myself, "All right, you've hit me, now get your glove out of my face."

As I dropped, I twisted my ankle. When I picked myself up off the canvas, I was unable to put any weight on it. The referee saw the look in my crossed eye and mercifully stopped it in the second round.

I still had a good record, though, with many, many more

wins than losses on the books. I had a good reputation for knowing how to fight, too, but everyone in the fight game knew something had happened to me during my fight with Gonzalez that left me only a shell of what I used to be. I would never be a contender again.

By then, I was considered a good test for a manager's up-and-coming prospect, but nothing more.

Greg Augustine called on me again. This time, he wanted to know if I wanted to fight in Hawaii. The fight card was going to be held in the Hula Bowl for the American soldiers returning from the Desert Storm war. Tommy Hearns was promoting it and was going to fight on the show himself. It was going to pay two thousand five hundred dollars, and all expenses. Since I was almost at poverty level, I agreed to the fight. I was to fight Anthony Hembrick, a gold medalist in the 1992 Olympic Games.

In the dressing room before the fight, one of Hembrick's trainers came up to me and said, "You look like you're in pretty good shape, Rusty. Are you sure you haven't fought in a while?"

"I always stay in good shape," I told him, "and I know how to fight. I'll guarantee you one thing, he's going to know he was in a fight."

Hembrick's trainer lowered his head and walked away, saying nothing.

At fight time, the stadium was about half full of soldiers. The bell rang, and we started feeling each other out by throwing jabs and moving on our feet. I backed myself into a corner to get a double-vision look at Anthony. He threw a jab-right hand combination. I blocked the jab, and the right hand fell short of its intended mark, my chin.

I began dancing out of the corner. Then, I saw a white towel come flying into the ring out of my corner, stopping the fight. I protested briefly, but it didn't take me long to realize that it was all set up. They were building up this kid's record for his future in the professional ranks, and I was a steppingstone. They didn't want their kid hurt.

I went back home, and my luck continued to run lousy. My grandmother was on her last leg of life and moved in with my mother. She agreed to give me three thousand dollars out of her life savings to open my own carpeting store.

Timing in life is everything. Like I mentioned earlier, I had spent most of my time at the hospital with my dying son. I did what I could with the time and the finances I had to clean an old rundown building I found and try to make it look presentable enough to sell carpet and linoleum out of.

The place had a nice-sized showroom. I carpeted it, putting some sample racks in the showroom. It turned out to be presentable enough to get some customers in and shopping.

I tried to get my life together, but it was hard. I'd had my boxing career ripped out of my heart, and there was nothing I could do to get it back. My wife and I love our children, very much. Losing two boys, back-to-back, was a tragedy. It got to the point where I began to wonder what else could go wrong.

The phone rang one afternoon, and Greg had another fighting event lined up for me, if I wanted it. He told me that, this time, Prince Charles Williams, the Light Heavyweight Champion of the World, was putting on an exhibition in his hometown of Mansfield, Ohio. From where I lived, that was about a two-hour drive. The Prince's management agreed to pay for gas, feed me dinner before the show and put me up in a hotel. They wanted me there a day in advance, and would pay me two hundred and fifty dollars to fight him three rounds wearing sixteen-ounce gloves and headgear.

That was like the "Godfather" making me an offer I couldn't refuse.

My brother-in-law, Stephen Adams, made the trip with me. We arrived safely and checked into our hotel. The Prince had a mini press conference the morning of the show during breakfast. He and I started sharing fight stories and actually bonded, I thought. I asked him if I could get one of the T-shirts displaying his name and picture on the front of the shirt.

He replied, "No problem, I'll get you one after the show tonight."

He and I got along for a bit. We drove around town all afternoon together. He seemed to be a very nice, classy champion of the world. We stopped at various places, and everyone knew him. He even took me with him to get his hair cut at his favorite barber.

As they say, though, all good things must come to an end. That night, that end came at fight time.

Here was the deal: there were two sparring partners fighting the prince. I chose to fight first. I was going to fight him three three-minute rounds then get out, and this other fellow was going to spar him three three-minute rounds. Remember, it was just an exhibition—no winners, no losers, it was just a sparring match.

I was on during this particular night, I mean, I was sharp. My eye was working, or at least it seemed to be. I tore Mr. Williams up. I hit him with hard body shots; I hit him with uppercuts to his protected chin followed by left hooks that landed with a loud thud on his headgear. He wore a full-face mask headgear. I couldn't have made direct contact with his face if I wanted to, and I wanted to.

When my three rounds were complete, the announcer said, "Let's give Rusty a big hand for a job well done."

With that, the viewing audience got up out of their seats and gave me a standing ovation. What a feeling!

Back to reality once again. It was the other guy's turn to spar the Prince three three-minute rounds. Only, the Prince looked as though he had just fought a twelve-round championship fight and lost. He changed the format: he would fight this other guy three rounds, all right, but changed it to three two-minute rounds.

The show ended, and everyone was leaving the auditorium. Many of the spectators shook my hand, telling me what great job I had done. The Prince walked up with his entourage. I extend my hand in friendship, but he turned his head and attempted to walk by me with his people.

I asked him, "What about that T-shirt you promised me?"

He stopped, grabbed a T-shirt from one of his friends (an extra T-shirt that didn't sell during the show), threw it at me, turned and walked away into the future. He never spoke another word to me. I guess I embarrassed him or something. Sorry, Prince. I'm an honest competitor. It was nothing personal.

One of the neighborhood kids came into the carpet store every day I was there, and we became friends. Danny Vigorito was twelve years old at the time. In a spare room off the main showroom, I had hung up a heavy bag and speed bag and brought in a weight bench and weights. During slow times of the day, which there were many, I'd work out.

Danny watched me hitting the bags and showed interest. I began teaching him boxing techniques. He caught on very quickly; and before I knew it, he was throwing punches like a real pro. Danny told and showed other kids in his neighborhood what I'd taught him, and in a short period of time I had five or six neighborhood kids coming in to my store to learn boxing moves.

The kids who showed up on a daily basis started to get in great shape. Their muscles got tighter and toned, they were losing excess fat, their confidence grew and they were more relaxed, easy-going.

One day, one of the kids said to me, "Rusty, that's a great idea you have, this 'Boxercise.' Have you ever advertised in the newspaper?"

This was in 1989.

I had to admit that I hadn't advertised. I contacted my friend, the sports writer for the *Warren Tribune* newspaper, Larry Ringler. I told him of my new fitness program called "Boxercise," what it was and some of the benefits people would experience if they stayed with the program. Larry found my new fitness concept to be interesting, and assigned a reporter to meet with me at my store to do an interview and photo shoot.

The following day there was a nice picture and lengthy story on my past boxing history and my new Boxercise program, offering it to anyone in the world who has a desire to get into shape and learn boxing techniques, all for only five dollars a workout.

* * *

Rusty? Then Boxercise
The Tribune Chronicle
Saturday, March 4, 1989

Rusty Rosenberger, a former Golden Gloves champion and professional boxer, will give a free demonstration of his Boxercise workout program at the Eastwood Mall in Niles.

The sessions will run from noon until 4:00 PM Saturday and Sunday near the Carlisle's entrance in the mall. The public is invited to watch and/or participate in the workouts. Rosenberger, a Niles resident,

> *describes Boxercise as a non-contact, cardiovascular workout, which teaches boxing techniques within an exercise routine. He says participants utilize almost every muscle in your body.*

* * *

The response was almost immediate. The phone at Rusty's Floor Store started to ring. I had a storeful of clients in a matter of days.

I thought that, since the *Warren Tribune* only reached people in the Warren-Niles area, if I could persuade the *Youngstown Vindicator* to do a story on my program, I'd be reaching twice as many people.

Because of my boxing background and numerous boxing articles in the paper done on my previous fights, it was easy to get the sports editor of the *Vindicator* to do a story on Boxercise. The *Vindicator* also took a photo of a student and me working out on the hand pads/focus mitts, and ran it in their newspaper.

It worked. I was really busy being a personal trainer for people from Trumbull and Mahoning counties. I was even getting some carpet sales from all the traffic my Boxercise was generating.

It was ironic, though. With all these people wanting to learn Boxercise and me teaching it, I again got the itch. I wanted to try one more time to accomplish my long-time dream of becoming a world champ or, at the very least, make enough money to build my wife that home I had promised her years ago. Living in a three-bedroom mobile home with three growing boys—we had two more sons by this time—was rough.

I started calling Greg Augustine every day, sometimes twice a day, until he finally lined me up a fight in

Columbus at the Columbus Convention Center. My opponent was a guy by the name of Kemper Morgan. He had fought Tommy Hearns and got iced a couple months prior.

To help me get ready for this fight, I found a sparring partner. His name was Mark Thomas, and he was the best I could do, given my financial circumstances. When he was only three years old a piece of metal had flown out from his father's lawnmower and hit him in the head, leaving him paralyzed on his right side.

Mark and I sparred; but I threw punches only to his body, and he tried to hit me if he could. Yes, I know that wasn't very good training tactics; but as I said, he was the best I could find in my circumstances.

The closest gym for me to go to was in Youngstown, which is a half-hour drive. There and back would have used more gas money than I had at the time, and I'm not sure my car could have traveled that far without breaking down. So, Mark and I boxed ten rounds every day for two weeks leading up to the fight.

Mark and I drove, using my dad's work truck, to Columbus the day before the match, and we were put up in a hotel room for the night. That next day I had to go be weighed in. I stepped on the scales, and it read one hundred seventy pounds.

Kemper was standing right beside me as I was on the scale; and as soon as he saw and heard the official call out my weight, he let out a loud moan and started taking off all of his clothes. The weight limit was one hundred seventy-five' and by the looks of him, he was well over the limit.

Kemper got on the scale, and the official pushed the weight indicator to one hundred seventy-five. Without the balance bar balancing itself on one hundred seventy-five, the official called out, "Morgan, one seventy-five," pushed the weight indicator back to zero and said, "Next."

During the fight, I was doing well—landing nice combinations and fighting inside strong. The only thing that I wasn't doing was slipping his long-armed jab. I couldn't see it coming, and he hit me repeatedly with it.

We fought the six rounds, and I lost it on a unanimous decision. I told my worried and concerned wife that I'd fight no more. I was now officially retired. A man has to know his limitations, and I had tried long and hard; but it was over—I was finished.

I feel that if Lou Duva hadn't given me those so-called blood-clotting pills, even with the fast and massive weight loss, I still would have beaten Nino. I feel that I would have realized my destiny as World Middleweight Champ, *guaranteed*!

* * *

Another one of my clients from Youngstown used to play football for the Wolverines of Michigan State. He had set a bench press record while in college. He lifted almost five hundred pounds during preseason one year. His name was Bobby Tabishino, and they called him "Tabby."

He was a mountain of a man. I trained him until his father helped me get a real job as a treatment agent for the Mahoning County Sheriff's Department in the jail division. I was employed there for about eight months, long enough to have been covered by insurance and to have the opportunity to get my eye surgically fixed. I had the operation in 1991.

I awoke from the sedation with great expectations. I was hoping that my eyes would again work together instead of seeing the same object in two different locations. I still had hopes of fighting and reaching my goal I had set for myself some fifteen years earlier. After a long recovery period, I found that the surgeon did move my eye muscle, but he didn't move it far enough. Now, I see two objects in different places in my mind's eye.

A month after the operation to my eye, again I lost my job due to budget cuts.

Before I took the job at the county, the state representative for Trumbull County, Michael Verich, had been working out in my Boxercise program with me. During one of our numerous workout sessions, he informed me of a state-funded prison that was being constructed in Leavittsburg, Ohio. He promised me he'd do what he could to get me an application for employment at the prison. He told me it would be up to me to pass the written test and the personal interview of a three-man board panel.

I figured he was just another politician making hopeful promises as politicians do.

Through the grapevine, I received word that the construction of the prison was complete and that they were going to start hiring staff to run the facility. I called Mr. Verich every Monday and Friday for at least two months straight. I bugged him unendingly. When we'd talk, I'd constantly remind him of his promise that he had made to me.

Finally, he got me an application for employment. I filled it out the same day I received it and sent it off to Columbus. A few weeks later, I received notice that a written exam would be given, and I was included for testing. I think it was kind of ironic that the testing site was going to be at the Packard Music Hall. The last time I had been in there, I was boxing.

I passed the test—in fact, I scored one of the highest scores of anyone taking the test on that day. I got an interview shortly thereafter, did well and was hired to work at the Trumbull Correctional Institution in Leavittsburg on December 14, 1992.

My wife and three boys had a good reason to be happy

that Christmas. I finally had a good job with benefits for my growing family. I was happy, too, but the thoughts of what I would have achieved in my life if Lou Duva hadn't told me to take those pills lingered.

I thought all my bad luck was behind me. Wrong. I was a well-known sports figure in the area. Oftentimes, I'd just be standing there talking to a staff member, from a corrections officer (CO) to the major, and they'd throw their hands up in the air and proceed to shadow box with me—briefly, of course. I've been fighting for over twenty years; it was a natural reaction to respond by shadow boxing back with them.

The warden and inmates saw this occurrence on many occasions, and before too long the inmates started shadow boxing with me, also. The warden, James Shotten, had advised me on several occasions not to shadow box with the staff, and especially the inmates.

Some time later, while in one of the housing units inside the prison walls—actually, it's two fifteen-foot-high fences with razor ribbon around the tops—I was doing a routine cell/shakedown inspection. I was looking for any contraband that an inmate might have had, like drugs or shanks—homemade knives.

As a CO, we are required to do at least three shakedown/cell searches each eight-hour shift we're working. When I was walking out of the cell, this big, muscular black inmate stepped in the doorway, blocking my exit.

He asked me, "What are you doing in my cell, Rosenberg?"

"A shakedown," I told him. "Excuse me," and attempted to walk out of the cell.

For no apparent reason, he balled his hand into a fist and punched me right in my solar plexus. It was if I had an X on my stomach. It landed perfectly and knocked almost all of the wind out of me.

In a flash, thinking about what the warden had told me over and over again about shadow boxing with the inmates, thinking *He'll never believe this guy hit me first*, I absorbed the punch and its effects on me. Trying not to look hurt, though I was, I stood up straight to face this inmate who had just assaulted me.

He threw another punch, right to the solar plexus again, knocking any remaining air out of my lungs. If I had had anything in my bowels, I would have actually not been able to hold it.

I unfolded my bent-over body once again to see this black man zeroing in on me again. I threw a right hand to his chest, which backed him off me for the moment. He launched a third left uppercut, hitting me exactly where the first two punches had landed. My face had to be beet-red from holding my breath.

Not being able to breathe, I sucked it up, looked him in the eyes and told him, "You won this round, champ."

I then went back to the officer's desk to lick my wounds.

A couple days went by, and this same inmate came up to the desk to talk to me. He told me that when he was released he was going to look me up and come visit me. He then said to me, "Yeah, I want to meet your whole family."

That sent a chill right through my bones. This guy had been in prison for the last eighteen years for a murder/rape. It was a life sentence, but he would become eligible for parole after serving twenty years. I was afraid of what this man might do to my beautiful wife and children.

All I could think about was being at work, locked inside a prison, when this man came to my house while I wasn't home to protect my family. I was going crazy. I had to make sure he never carried out his threat.

The only thing I could think of was to write up an incident report and hope he'd get sentenced for two more years for assaulting an officer.

I turned in my report and was called before the warden for an interview. I told him the truth about this incident, word for word. Then the warden called for the inmate and asked him what his version was.

The inmate lied, turning the whole story around. He told Mr. Shotten that it was I who hit him. The warden believed the inmate, because of my boxing background, and arranged to get him an early parole instead of pressing charges against the state.

The warden had me removed my position as a CO. He had me fired. I lost my paycheck and the insurance benefits for my family. Being a fighter by nature, I fought it.

There are six steps in the union process, It took the union six months to get a trial on my behalf; I was forced to take it all the way into litigation. The case went before an arbitrator; and, when I told him the truth, my version, he believed me and awarded me my job back. I didn't receive any back pay, but I got my job back.

Still, I was really sweating. The inmate had been paroled to Youngstown. He was so close to where I lived that I couldn't help but worry about my family's safety. It wasn't a week after his parole, though, that the man was picked up in Youngstown driving a stolen car with no license plate and no driver's license, with a gun under the front seat and some kind of illegal drugs in his possession. That violated his parole. Quick as a flash, he was back in the Ohio's prison system for another five years. Thank you, God, thank you!

CHAPTER 15

Destiny Unfolds

I still have the heart of a champion, and the desire to prove to the world somehow that I was destined to be a world champion. My body is no longer capable of going twelve rounds in the ring with a man half my age, but I've still found ways to stay active in the sport.

I train men and women, young adults and children in my Boxercise program. I've done so for the past twelve years, including the entire time the state of Ohio has employed me as a corrections officer and, currently, as a sergeant, during my days off and after work.

I surf the Internet looking for boxing sites. When I find one, I send my business card via email. The card shows a picture of me wearing a pair of boxing gloves and gives a description of my Boxercise program. I offer the benefits one would obtain working out in the program.

I also wrote a true story about "The True...Lou Duva," telling of his underhanded tactics. I emailed that story off to newspapers, magazines, attorneys, authors, ghostwriters—any email address I could find. I hoped someone would understand the pain and suffering I endure to this very day. I've been trying all these years to find a way for the world to hear my story.

I received an email in response to my Lou Duva story

and agreed to do a phone interview with a man from Canada by the name of Mike Talbot, who was then working for "Slam! Boxing."

The following is a result of our conversation:

Rusty's Rocky Road

Someone once told me that you can play hockey, you can play soccer and you can play baseball...but you can't play boxing. In a world that far too often seems cold and cruel, boxing is reality's sport.

And for every Oscar de la Hoya or Shane Mosley that graces a magazine cover with a million-dollar smile, there is a man like Rusty Rosenberger. An ex-fighter, long forgotten, light-years away from fleeting glory, struggling to put a sentence together, unable to play catch with his children because he sees two of everything. You don't hear about the Rusty Rosenbergers, but they exist. They are what is harsh and what is real about the gloriously violent, magnificently brutal world of pugilism.

I received an email from Rusty Rosenberger quite some time ago. I skimmed through it, not quite sure what to make of it. The gist of what I got out of it was that he was a promising contender who had been wronged, been exploited and battered, left with a permanently damaged brain, double vision and a bad taste in his mouth. But mostly, he was left with the frustrating thoughts of what could have been—had things been different. But they weren't different and life is cruel. I thought about deleting that email and in doing so adding a little muscle to a collective sweep under the carpet, but something prevented me from doing so.

I emailed Rusty back and we agreed to a phone interview. He seemed excited that I had responded. He closed out his email with a p.s.: "I do talk like a punch drunk fighter."

I called Rusty the next day. A woman answered. A child was burning energy in the background. I taped our conversation. I tried my hardest to listen to his story, but after a minute or two I realized it was futile. I felt truly sorry for Rusty Rosenberger and I hope he understands that I am in no way mocking him when I say I had a difficult time understanding him that day. When I got off the phone with him, I felt a blast of coldness. The world seemed cruel and unforgiving. I couldn't understand what Rusty was telling me, but I could hear the hurt in his voice and the embarrassment. I could sense the fighter's pride and I knew he was living with a cruel fate.

I didn't think I had much of a story. Rusty emailed and apologized for his slurred speech. Like his previous email, the little tiny tape of our phone conversation laid dormant for quite a few days. Every night when I wrote at my desk in my basement apartment, I looked at it and wondered: just a tiny little tape, I thought, but someone's story, someone's life. I was tempted to sweep it all away again, do the easy thing and let it rot under a cowardly carpet. Chalk it up to hard luck and frigid reality. But instead I listened to it—for hours. Rewound it and listened to it again until I understood every word that he was saying. And when I did, I sat with eyes wide and my mouth gaping as a fantastic story unfolded, word by laborious word. I could hardly believe what I was hearing.

It was a story about boxing and bad luck, about being ripped off by the vultures he trusted. It was about organized crime and gambling, about being drugged before fights. About missed opportunities and beatings. About being set up and pummeled. About being forced to lose ridiculous amounts of weight on short notice. About regrets, and anger. About a well-known figure in the boxing world who was in debt with the wrong people and used Rusty like a piece of bloody meat to dig himself out of a hole. It was about greed and evil, violence and betrayal.

But more than anything, it was about not giving up. It was about a man named Rusty Rosenberger, 1979 New Jersey State Middleweight Champion, who took the hardest knocks the world could throw and stayed on his feet. A man who told me, "Mike, I live every day walking around this world with my head cocked to the right. The reason I do this is so I see one object in front of me instead of two." But Rusty didn't lie down and die. He claims to have invented

Boxercise, but didn't have the money or the backing to patent it. Unfazed, he invented body boxing, a safe alternative to boxing in which opponents target only the area between the shoulders and the waist. Three two-minute rounds in a regulation size ring with eighteen-ounce gloves. No brain damage. No double vision.

In the end, I was inspired and extremely interested in his tragic story. When I listened to that tape, I realized that Rusty was a brave warrior, and I realized that the fight was not knocked out of him when he was allegedly drugged and took a savage beating at the hands of Nino Gonzalez. His language may be slurred, but his mind works just fine. He is a man with ideas and ambitions and I'm glad I got to know him. It makes me wonder how many times we've taken the easy road and swept a guy like Rusty under the carpet because we couldn't be bothered or didn't have the time. No matter, a true fighter like Rusty Rosenberger can't be held down. Not when the heart of a champion pounds inside his chest. Not when he was born to fight.

Mr. Shotten was transferred to another facility, and Trumble Correctional Institute got a new warden to replace him. Our new warden was an African-American woman—a woman in charge of an all-male close security prison?. When I first met this woman and we shook hands, I had to do a double-take to make sure I was shaking hands with a woman. She had the grip of a man. I even commented on her powerful handshake and she smiled. I felt we had made something of a bond.

Again, I was wrong. As time went by, she became distant and unfriendly towards me. I suspect she may have drawn the conclusion that I was stupid based solely on my punch-drunk speech. It must have offended her.

After she took over, the executives in the DR&C in Columbus put out an order to check all employees' applications for any untruthful documentation. There had been a crop of people who had blatantly lied on their applications. Mine was one of the applications that were brought into question.

On my application, where it asks for the highest degree or level obtained under education, I wrote that I had "two years assc. in business." I had attended Youngstown State University for two years. Nowhere on my application did I indicate or even suggest I had a degree or diploma. What I meant by writing "two years assc. in business" was I was associated with business for two years, not that I had a two-year associates degree or diploma.

I was fired again, this time for four months. Once this misunderstanding was cleared up, I was again reinstated at Trumbull, this time as a CO.

My Boxercise was becoming a big hit in Niles, the town I live in. I'd started teaching my program at a local fitness center called Ron Crawford's World of Fitness. It had all the latest equipment, from treadmills to weights, and offered aerobics, karate and, now, Boxercise. The clientele were mostly men, with a few ladies mixed in.

One of my most consistent clients was a big, burly man by the name of Bob Granny. He has a left hook that could knock out a buffalo. He stands six feet, two inches tall, weighs two hundred twenty-five pounds, all solid muscle, and is fifty-five years old. He is also one of the nicest guys I have ever met in all my travels.

We were actually sparring to the head one day at the gym. We were in the middle of the third round when he told me he was tired and needed a break. I always motivate my clients never to give up until the bell rings to end the round, but right in the middle of the round, he wanted a break.

I told him, no-no, the round's not over yet. He insisted that we take a break. I wasn't ready to give up, though. I put my hands down at my side, danced up close to him and said, "Are you giving up? That makes you a loser! Come on, let's finish the round."

In an instant, he unleashed a powerful left hook, right on the money, to my jaw. I saw stars for a moment. From that day on, I nicknamed him "The Possum."

After Big Bob rang my bell for me, I decided I didn't need to be hit in the head anymore. I still enjoyed the combativeness, the conditioning, the camaraderie of training with another athlete and, of course, boxing; but I didn't think it was worth getting my skull caved in more. After all, I couldn't see the punches coming, since I was seeing double constantly.

Later that same day, after I had gotten home, I sat down and thought over my Boxercise program and how I could intensify the workout to be even more comparable to boxing without the dangerous aspect of being hit in the head.

Then, my wife walked in the room, and I stood up to greet her. In a playful mood, she threw a punch to my stomach and said, "Hi."

The idea of fighting just to the body went off in my brain like fireworks.

I immediately called Bob and scheduled another workout. It was great. All the elements of boxing are there: technique, conditioning, control, endurance, footwork, blocking punches—everything you can think of was incorporated into this new type of workout, except the dangers involved by being struck in the head or face. No black or cut eyes, no broken or bloody noses and, especially, no brain damage.

What would I call this new type of competition? I considered a few different titles and came up with "BodyBoxing."

My male clients loved it. We trained like this for about six months. When we were BodyBoxing at the gym, there'd always be a crowd of spectators. I had another idea. Maybe, if I were to promote a BodyBoxing show, people might enjoy coming out to watch their friends or family members boxing safely.

There would be a regulation-size ring, with a referee, three judges, a timekeeper, a bell and a ring card girl. Each fighter would wear eighteen-ounce gloves, a mouthpiece and a protective cup. There would be a trophy for the winner and the runner-up and T-shirts with the logo "Rusty's BodyBoxing" on the front for everyone who participated.

My first show wasn't as well-attended as I'd hoped. The bill for the show came to about a thousand dollars. I went to a few businesses in town and got donations, telling them that, between rounds, I'd have my ring announcer read from their business cards to give them some advertisement. Most of the bill was footed by a friend/client, a surgeon in Warren, Ohio, by the name of Dr. Fitzpatrick.

As I sat and watched my first-ever production, I thought about when I was the star, the champ, undefeated and heading for a world boxing title. How exciting life was then. The production ended; and as I came back to reality, I found that those times were somehow a little closer.

A few months later I almost had more guys BodyBoxing than I could train. When I trained them, I'd fight them, all of them, one after another. At times there were five or six guys in my garage fighting me. I would spar one after another, sometimes doing as many as twenty-five three-minute rounds. I truly loved it. Again, it's the closest thing to real fighting that you can get, and I loved to fight.

My second show had a great lineup of fighters. With big Ken Pleviyak—at six-foot-four, he's two hundred thirty-five pounds of muscle and works as a concrete finisher. His technique needed refining, but his strength and punching power were almost superhuman. His punches came from left and right field like a whirlwind, and when they landed they were solid.

I matched him up against Dave Hanshaw, a man with beautiful techniques, fast fists, strength and fantastic footwork.

When I would train clients at the health club, and Dave was scheduled at five-thirty, he'd show up at five o'clock and just sit there and watch how I moved on my feet. Then, I'd work him out and teach him what I could. Before long, he danced like a champ. He owns the biggest set of calf muscles I've ever seen, and he used them to his benefit.

I had the tournament set up where the champ from my first show was automatically seeded to the finals. In the heavyweight division there were four fighters. Dave won his first two fights back-to-back, and then had to fight big Ken in the finals.

What a fight! Ken threw some powerful roundhouse rights and lefts that wore Dave down. Dave fought back with a true champion's heart, but Ken was fresh and powerful, knocking Dave around the ring like a punching bag. In the end, it was Big Ken Pleviyak walking away with the champion's trophy.

The main event was an attorney by the name of Lou Guannari from Warren, Ohio, who is now the prosecuting attorney for Stark County, Ohio, going up against a very tough competitor, a coworker of mine, a corrections officer named Craig Furness, from Ravenna, Ohio. They both weighed in at one hundred sixty pounds.

It was a tough fight. In the first round, they both came out firing some tremendous body shots. The leather was making sounds like gunshots when they connected. At the start of the second, things looked very even. Both fighters fired combinations and moved well on their feet until Furness landed a hard right hand to the jaw of Lou, dropping him like a bad habit.

After giving Lou about five minutes to recuperate and get his senses back, the referee deducted one point for the head shot and the fight continued. What a pace these two warriors were fighting at. In all my years of boxing, I've never seen a pace of such intensity before. These two fighters were in great physical condition—they had to be, fighting nonstop like they were.

When the dust settled and the fight was over, the crowd roared and came to its feet. The decision was given to Lou Guanneri, winning by one point on all the judges' scorecards. They both were winners that evening.

This was all well and good, except I wanted that feeling of being in the spotlight again. I remember how special I'd feel in front of thousands of people. The only feeling that even came close—and it was better—was the thrill and joy of watching my wife give birth to each of our six boys. Somehow, I needed to get it back.

I think Lou Duva made a fortune for himself at my expense. I believe he destroyed my outstanding boxing career, ruined my eyesight and literally killed my chances of ever achieving my destiny as the World Middleweight Champ. Well, he may have taken this fighter out of the competitive boxing ring, but he'll never take the fighter out of me. *Never!*

Back at TCI, things still weren't going well for me. There was a posting for a sergeant's position. At the time, the State of Ohio Department of Rehabilitation and Corrections' policy was one of promoting by seniority. I held the highest seniority of all the applicants who put in for the promotion. I should have been promoted to the sergeant's position.

Instead, the DRC passed me over and gave it to an African-American with less seniority time. Our union president, George Adamrovich, put up one hell of a show of disapproval; and, after four months of negotiating on my behalf, he finally did get me my promotion. By that time, we had another warden; his name was Julius Wilson.

One warm summer day, while walking across the prison yard on a paved walkway eating a juicy plum, I bent over forward while I walked—I didn't want the juice from the plum dripping on my white uniform shirt.

I stepped in an uneven part of the walkway and stumbled briefly, losing my balance. My luck continued. The warden just happened to be looking out his office window. He could see the entire prison facility from that window; and as my luck would once again have it, he witnessed me stumbling.

At lunchtime, I entered the chow hall and saw Captain Tim Franklin on the phone talking. As I walked by him, I overheard him say, "And it's getting progressively worse."

I just knew he meant me.

When he finished his conversation and hung up the phone, I asked him whom he talked to and if he was referring to me. At first he denied it, but, being persistent, I asked him again. Finally, showing the kind of integrity that any state prison would want in its captains, he admitted that he was talking about me to the warden.

"What did you say during your conversation?" I asked.

"The warden saw you stumble from his high perch," he said, "and is concerned about your stability."

"You told him that my walking ability and balance is getting progressively worse?"

"Yes, I did," he said. "Over the last couple of years, I've

noticed you trip and stumble more than once."

"You're entitled to your own opinion," I said, "but you're wrong. If anything, I've become more aware of my disability and work on improving it on a daily basis."

Twenty-five years after that fight at Giants Stadium, I still suffer the effects of the beating. The damage to my right eye is beyond repair. After two eye surgeries, my right eye still drifts to the right, making it difficult at times for me to keep my balance when I walk. Often, it appears as though I'm drunk.

To play catch with one of my four growing young boys is impossible. I can't determine how close the ball is to me or at what level it's traveling. I almost always have to repeat what I have said—my voice is hard to understand.

The "Punch Drunk Syndrome" that I suffer day to day is tough to live with. It's a constant reminder of the injustice that Lou wreaked upon me in 1979.

Still, I refuse to quit trying to reclaim myself. Even at the age of forty-six, I still yearn for that big break in my life that will let the whole world know that I'm a champ and realize my destiny.

My BodyBoxing has taken a change of course. Instead of promoting the shows for other participants to fight, I now have "Fund Raiser Shows" featuring myself. For a fee, anyone, and I stress *anyone* can get in the ring and BodyBox a round with me. All proceeds are donated to a nonprofit organization.

My first fundraiser was held at the Trumbull County Fair in Bazzetta, Ohio, on July 15, 2000. Dan Polivka, a politician in Warren and one of the executive board members, not only used his influence to help me promote and coordinate such an event, he participated in the show himself. I raised one hundred fifty dollars at the fair, fighting fifteen consecutive rounds at ten dollars per round. The proceeds went to the Trumbull County 4-H Club.

The following summer, on July 3, 2001, at the Waddell Festival, held in Waddell Park, Niles, Ohio, I held my second benefit BodyBoxing show. This time, the proceeds were set to go to the Niles Red Dragons, the high school football team that my son played on.

I attended a few meetings of the Niles Frontliners, a group of fathers who try to raise money yearly for the football team's expenses. At one of the meetings, the executive board discussed ways to financially aid in the construction of a new locker room for the high school football team.

I spoke to Mike Dunn, the president of the Frontliners for that year. I told him that at the Fourth of July Festival that year I could put on a BodyBoxing show to try and raise money for the team. Mike put it out on the table in front of the Frontliners meeting to have it voted on. The verdict was unanimous: I could pursue such a fundraising event.

Time passed quickly, as it always does when I'm in training; and the Festival was underway almost before I knew it. There was a nice crowd on hand to watch me fight as many volunteers as I possibly could. The fee for fighting me one round was twenty dollars. For the hometown football team, I felt the fee to be appropriate.

I boxed sixteen rounds, making three hundred twenty dollars for the team. When one of the participants crawled in the ring with me, I couldn't believe my eyes. He looked like a Kodiak bear, not a human being. He weighed in at three hundred seventy-five pounds, a real monster of a man.

The bell rang, initiating the round; and here came this human iceberg. He tried very hard to hit me, but I dared not let him. He'd break me in half! Then, without warning, frustrated from not being able to hit me, he grabbed me by my shoulders and threw me into the ropes.

If he and I started wrestling, I'd definitely have been in

trouble, but we weren't, we were BodyBoxing. I hit the ropes, and the tension propelled me forward. I hit him with a right uppercut to his huge stomach, and I heard a loud *ohhh!*

He bent straight over, as if he were bowing to my boxing abilities. He recovered without further ado. We did talk later that day; and he said his stomach felt somewhat sore, but, other than that, he recovered. Sorry, big man, all done in fun.

On July 10, 2001, I held my third BodyBoxing benefit show. Dan Polivka invited me back to the Trumbull County Fair. I boxed fifteen consecutive rounds, again earning a total of one hundred fifty dollars for Trumbull County's 4-H Club.

Warden Julius Wilson tried to get me to leave my job by suggesting that I go out on Permanent Medical Disability. He felt that I was a risk working in a close-security prison setting. I checked into the possibility. The state requires you to have five years of uninterrupted service before you can collect the maximum amount of disability.

State employees pay into a retirement fund called the Public Employees Retirement System. When the state wrongfully fired me twice, I withdrew all of my retirement funds to feed my children and pay my bills. I have only paid back into the P.E.R.S. a total of two and a half years to date.

I told Mr. Wilson that I would consider retirement when I was able to receive the maximum amount for my services, if and when I decided to retire. I even went on an interview with the Civil Rights Commission, located in Akron, to file a possible lawsuit against the state and Warden Wilson for discrimination. Nothing came of my lawsuit, though Warden Wilson has not bothered me lately and I don't intend to give him any reason to do so.

My life didn't turn out the way I hoped it would.

Instead, I ended up securing a decent-paying job with good benefits and a beautiful family whom I love with all my heart. My wife and I did build a house to raise our boys in. It's not the mansion I would have been able to afford if my boxing career hadn't met Lou Duva; but, as they say, it's home.

My firstborn son, Scott, graduated from high school in 2002 and is enrolled in college at Youngstown State University. He earned straight A's his senior year in high school and is unquestionably an intelligent young man. I'm sure he'll do well in life.

Scott has a gift but does not have the drive to go after it. He is able to run with great speed over long distances. During football and baseball season, the teams ran laps around the track that circles the football field for conditioning. He lapped most of his teammates.

My second and third born, as you know, are in Heaven with God. I plan on seeing them again some time in the future.

Joshua, my fourth son, is a good athlete. He has huge, powerful hands that can build just about whatever he puts his mind to. I remember buying my boys a basketball hoop that needed to be assembled. As I looked over the confusing directions, he stepped back, looked at the picture on the box and had the hoop built in no time. If he puts his mind to becoming an athlete, no matter what sport he chooses, I know he'll be outstanding.

Danny, or "Peanut," as we call him, is my fifth son. He is the runt of the pack; but, wouldn't you know it, he's my best athlete out of them all so far. In baseball, he plays shortstop and makes big league plays. I tell him that if there were a professional Little League team he'd be on it. In basketball, he is super-quick. He won the Niles fifth-and sixth-grade one-on-one tournament without losing a game. In football, he is a great one-on-one open field tackler with speed of foot and moves that remind me of Barry Sanders.

Last but not least, there is Robbie. Currently, he is only five years old, but I just can tell he is special. He's smart, fast, strong and athletic. My other boys work with him on a daily basis, teaching him the fundamentals of basketball, football and baseball. He possesses a powerful upper body; and, yes, I've already taught him how to throw a punch, as I've taught all my boys.

During my boxing career, I had a powerful punch. Maybe Robbie inherited it. When this five-year-old kid punches me anywhere on my body, it hurts.

He has other talents, as well. When he was only three years old, I went to pick up my two boys at football practice. My mother, Helen, was watching Robbie for me, but as I drove up I didn't see him with her. I parked, walked up to her and asked where he was. Would you believe that he was running laps? He completed a mile run, doing the last lap right before my eyes. At the age of only three and a half, I found that to be remarkable.

Folks, remember that name, Robbie Rosenberger. He'll be special one day in the future.

That's my life up to date. I've had a lot of bad luck, but a lot of good, also. It's impossible for me to ever forget what I believe Lou Duva did to me in the prime of my boxing career, but that goes to show you that I refuse to give up and quit trying to live life to its fullest.

I love to train daily. I run; and when I run my black Doberman attached to his lead, which is connected to me by a belt, drags me around the development we live in. Or I'll run and hit my heavy bag for ten three-minute rounds, or run and workout on my Bow-Flex.

I usually do one or two of my programs daily. On the rare occasion I'll find someone to BodyBox with me. I'm going to turn forty-seven years old this August, and I have a resting heart rate of forty-five beats per minute, not bad for an old man.

I don't know what's in store for me the rest of my life, or how long that may be. One thing's for sure, though: I'll be in fighting shape for what comes my way.

Though I may not have reached my destiny as the World Middleweight Champ, I still fight with the heart of a champion.

Epilogue

On a warm spring evening in 2002, I picked up the phone and dialed Rusty's number. Things had been building up to this moment for a couple of weeks—a publisher I work for had recommended Rusty to me, we had corresponded and I'd gone over his story.

My name is Jeff Mullen, and I edit books professionally. On that night, though, I was a little nervous.

I don't know why, but I often have more trouble than most understanding people whose speech is slurred. It embarrasses me—not because I think I'm better than this person (I don't), but because I feel that I, with my big vocabulary and writing skills, should be able to do better.

Rusty, of course, had given me plenty of build-up about the way he speaks. I had heard half the stories about the "punch-drunk boxer" who couldn't put three clear words together. I was ready for a rough time.

His wife answered the phone and, after a few seconds, handed it to him, and that was when everything changed.

Rusty spoke with a gentle but excited voice. Though he was a little self-conscious at first, I never had any trouble understanding what he was saying. On the contrary, what I heard in that voice was a man very much in love with life and set on making a better future for himself and his family, despite whatever obstacles may be placed in his path.

I had been afraid that I might have run into a whiner, but what I found instead was inspiration.

Rusty hasn't led an easy life, but he's forged himself a living through hard work and determination. At an age where most men are thinking about winding down their lives, Rusty is still working hard on new prospects. At an age where many have given up on their bodies, Rusty is still working hard to keep his in good working order. I give him a lot of credit for that.

Rusty never found that ghostwriter he was looking for. He only found me. Rusty wrote this book, and I cleaned it up a little. Frankly, it was an easy book to edit—and I hope that it was just as easy to read.

Anybody who's thinking about a career in boxing should read this book. What was really in those pills? Horse tranquilizers? Valium? Only Lou Duva can answer that question, and he hasn't said a word about it in over ten years. No matter what it was, Lou used them to hurt a good man, a man he never had any business harming; and he never paid the price for his tomfoolery.

Rusty Rosenberger is a hero. He took the worst kind of beating that a man can take and came back for more. There were hundreds of times when he could have called it quits, and he got back up and found a way to go on. In this world, a man deserves a lot of credit for that.

I, for my part, am going to try to stay in touch with him. He has a lot to offer this world, and I'd like to know how he fares.

What does the future hold? Well, I just got off the phone with Rusty before I wrote this paragraph. He was very excited. It seems someone heard about his book and recommended it to a film studio. There's talk of a movie deal. I'm going to be sending the manuscript out myself, even though I won't be seeing a cent of the proceeds if the deal comes through. I, personally, can't think of a man on earth who would deserve it any more than Rusty. What does destiny have in store?

END

ABOUT RUSTY

Gregg "Rusty" Rosenberger was born to be a professional boxer. In 1979, after years of hard work and dedicated training, he became the New Jersey State Middleweight Champion, and a legitimate contender for the World Title. It seemed like destiny. Then, one night before a fight, his manager, Lou Duva, gave him some pills to take. After that fight, neither Rusty nor his career would ever be the same.

Rusty is a Sergeant working in an Ohio correctional facility. He's been married for nineteen years and has four wonderful, intelligent, athletic sons. He loves his family dearly, and thanks God for sending an angel named Cindy to watch over him.

At 47 years old, he still works out on an almost daily basis, staying in top shape. While he trains, thoughts of what could have been, what should have been, what WOULD have been never leaves his mind. He feels that it is important for others to know his story, to learn from his life.

27453507R10092

Printed in Poland
by Amazon Fulfillment
Poland Sp. z o.o., Wrocław